Putting Teachers First

M000276295

In *Putting Teachers First*, author and speaker Brad Johnson offers tons of invaluable tips for building and maintaining strong, dynamic relationships with your teachers, leading to greater job satisfaction, lower turnover, and improved performance across the board. You'll learn how to boost teacher morale and drive engagement by providing sincere feedback and recognition, creating incentives for teaching excellence, building trust between all faculty members, and more.

Topics covered:

♦ The Importance of Teacher Satisfaction
♦ Motivating Your Teachers to Succeed
♦ Creating a Culture of Appreciation
♦ Learning to Become a Selfless Leader
♦ Inspiring Teachers to Remember Their Purpose
♦ Developing Your Emotional Intelligence
♦ Communicating and Connecting Effectively
♦ Building a Cohesive Team
♦ Celebrating Successes

Each chapter includes practical advice as well as inspiring stories and anecdotes to motivate you on your journey.

Dr. Brad Johnson has over 20 years of experience as a teacher and administrator at the K–12 and collegiate level. He is a national speaker and author and is also on the national faculty for Concordia University School of Graduate Studies in Leadership. His other books include *Learning On Your Feet: Incorporating Physical Activity into the K–8 Classroom* and *From School Administrator to School Leader: 15 Keys to Maximizing Your Leadership Potential*.

Putting Teachers First

How to Inspire, Motivate, and Connect with Your Staff

Brad Johnson

Routledge
Taylor & Francis Group

NEW YORK AND LONDON

First published 2019
by Routledge
711 Third Avenue, New York, NY 10017

and by Routledge
2 Park Square, Milton Park, Abingdon, Oxon, OX14 4RN

Routledge is an imprint of the Taylor & Francis Group, an informa business

© 2019 Taylor & Francis

Library of Congress Cataloging-in-Publication Data
A catalog record for this book has been requested

ISBN: 978-1-138-58665-9 (hbk)
ISBN: 978-1-138-58667-3 (pbk)
ISBN: 978-0-429-50446-4 (ebk)

Typeset in Palatino
by Apex CoVantage, LLC

Contents

Meet the Author

Dr. Brad Johnson is one of the most dynamic and engaging speakers in the fields of education and leadership. He is author of *Learning On Your Feet: Incorporating Physical Activity into the K–8 Classroom* with Melody Jones, as well as *What Schools Don't Teach: 20 Ways to Help Students Excel in School and in Life* and *From School Administrator to School Leader: 15 Keys to Maximizing Your Leadership Potential*, both with Julie Sessions. He has over 20 years of experience as a teacher and administrator at the K–12 and collegiate level. Beyond speaking and writing, Dr. Johnson is on the national faculty for Concordia University School of Graduate Studies in Leadership.

1

The Importance of Teacher Satisfaction

Great teachers leave a legacy.
—Brad Johnson

There is no profession where job satisfaction is more important or has more far reaching impact than in teaching. If teachers aren't happy, it can be carried into the classroom and ultimately affect the whole learning culture of a classroom and school. There has been extensive research in the corporate world regarding the impact of job satisfaction on employees' work production, morale, and even the effects on personal life, but the teaching profession has failed to be a part of this important conversation. However, this doesn't mean that teacher job satisfaction is not important or that it can't be significantly improved when leaders make it a focus.

We have always been told the student comes first, and to the teacher this is true, but for the administration, teachers come first. When teachers feel like they matter, they not only affect students' lives positively, but they can affect their lives forever. What if our schools welcomed all their staff the way that Apple welcomes their employees? Here is the note that is given to Apple employees when they start with the company:

There's work and there's your life's work.
 The kind of work that has your fingerprints all over it.
The kind of work that you'd never compromise on. That you'd

sacrifice a weekend for. You can do that kind of work at Apple. People don't come here to play it safe. They come here to swim in the deep end.

Something big. Something that couldn't happen anywhere else.

Welcome to Apple.

What if you encouraged your teachers to put their fingerprints all over their work, to swim in the deep end, and to do something big? Put your teachers first and see how quickly the whole culture of the school will change and student achievement will soar.

What Affects Job Satisfaction?

Many factors affect job satisfaction, such as pay, autonomy, planning time, and even support from administration. And one of the biggest influences on job satisfaction among teachers as we will see throughout the book deals with feeling valued, having input into decision making, and developing strong positive relationships with their administration.

Lack of Resources

Teachers continually deal with lack of resources, especially in lower socio economic districts. But even in more affluent areas, teachers don't have the same access to resources to perform their jobs as employees of a local business, for example. In the corporate world, there is an expectation that you will have every resource necessary to perform your job effectively, but this is not the case in education.

One example of a teacher struggling with job satisfaction due to lack of resources is an Oklahoma educator, Teresa Danks Roark. She has even become a celebrity of sorts. The reason was not that she was named teacher of the year, had high standardized test scores, or even created some interesting project for her students, but that she was out panhandling on the highways of Oklahoma. Yes, a veteran teacher with a master's degree was on the side of the road begging for money. Teresa wasn't asking for the money for herself, but for her students. She said that budget cuts in the state had left supply levels even lower than usual. She said that she typically spends about $2,000–$3,000.00 of her own salary each year on supplies and that she felt like it was time to make the public more aware of the lack of funding in schools. In an email interview with us, Teresa shared a little of her experience.

> I knew I wanted a photo for social media and that I was doing it to make a point about how bad it is in public education today. However, the public did not know the facts. As teachers, we are forced to do more with less, it really does create a negative environment where job satisfaction and motivation suffer greatly. If I can't even get the resources I need to do my job effectively, am I really valued as a teacher and a professional? So, I decided to create a sign and go out on the highway and basically beg for money to do my job. As the light turned red, I became very nervous. I had a no idea how people were going to react to me standing out there "panhandling." I wondered if they would shame me with words or even worse throw things at me. I had no idea what was coming.
>
> However, my belief in what I was doing gave me the courage to take the risk. I feel that public awareness and public support is so important in order to create real change. As it turned out, I experienced the total opposite of what I had feared. I became overwhelmed by the outpouring of love and generosity from the public. Then, one stranger literally took me to tears. It was a young woman who handed me a few one dollar bills, her tips for the day, while saying "a teacher like you is why I am alive today." That was it. I knew at that moment, this was so much bigger than me and my classroom needs. I went home, and posted the picture. About an hour later I was contacted by local media and the story took off. After receiving hundreds of emails and messages from

teachers across the state and the nation, I knew I had to fight for all teachers and the children we serve.

While this may seem like an extreme case, there are teachers all around the country creating GoFundMe accounts to raise money for their classrooms. They are in essence panhandling as well, but aren't standing on the highway to do it. In what other profession would you see people resort to begging or "panhandling" just to do their job more effectively? And limited supplies is just one of the many challenges faced by teachers and as challenges mount, they greatly affect teacher job satisfaction and motivation in the classroom.

Teachers Aren't Viewed as Professionals

In our Teachers First survey that we sent out to teachers around the country, one of their responses to increasing job satisfaction was to be seen as professionals by their administration and especially by parents and their communities. One reason that teachers may not be viewed as professionals is that teaching is often seen as a "calling" rather than as a profession, which is a way of saying that teachers are born and that teaching doesn't really require rigorous training beyond knowing the subject being taught.

While teaching may be a calling for some, it is a profession to all that requires rigorous academic training, student teaching experiences, certification/licensing, and continual professional development to maintain certification. This sounds like a profession and until teaching is seen as a profession, teachers will continue to endure a culture where teaching is not respected to the level that it should be.

When teaching is viewed solely as a calling, it gives the connotation of a servant rather than a servant leader. So teachers are often expected to be accepting of lower pay, increase in workload, and lower job satisfaction all under the motto that "students come first." They feel compelled to spend their own money on supplies, or even panhandle on the highway because they are often left to fend for themselves for their classroom needs.

The sentiment that teaching is not really a profession is deeply immersed in our culture. According to Richard Ingersoll of the University of Pennsylvania,

> We do not refer to teaching as a profession. It doesn't have the characteristics of those traditional professions like medicine, academia, dentistry, law, architecture, engineering, et cetera. It doesn't have the pay, the status, the respect, the length of training, so from a scientific viewpoint teaching is not a profession.
>
> (Ingersoll, 2001, 15)

While the pay and status of teaching is not on the level of other professions, it is noteworthy to share that 56% of all teachers have a master's degree or higher and with state certification requirements, teachers have training that is comparable to other professions.

Another point made by Ingersoll is that one hallmark of a profession is longevity, sticking with the work. In that respect, teaching doesn't make the grade. As noted earlier, his research indicates that at least 40% of new teachers leave the field within five years, a rate of attrition that is comparable to police work. However, there are several factors which make this number skewed. For instance, most new teachers are females in their early twenties. This means they are at a life stage where they may marry and begin families. So, part of the attrition has nothing to do with teaching itself. But the number is high enough to cause concern.

Why is it a big deal that teachers are viewed and treated as professionals? How often are teachers expected to work long hours, spend their own money on classroom materials, or to fall in line with the latest program "no questions asked" because it is all about the students? As many teachers responded in our survey, "we continually have more added to our plate, but nothing is ever taken from our plate." Teachers overwhelmingly replied that part of their low job satisfaction is the fact that they aren't treated as a professional.

Have you wondered why teachers in Finland, South Korea, and other high-performing countries are seen as professionals and in turn have higher job satisfaction than teachers in the US? It is in part due to the fact that teachers are viewed as the experts and it is their expertise that drives curriculum and teaching. And the administration is there to support their experts by creating a positive school culture. In the US, education is used as a pawn by politicians, who are not teachers, but who develop policies for education. Teachers are rarely given a voice and have very little control over decisions that directly affect their ability to do their job.

Putting Teachers First: Lesson from the Corporate World

While the concept of putting teachers first may seem like a strange concept, effective corporate leaders have used it for decades. This is not to say that the student isn't important, but the phrase "students first" is so engrained into our thinking that to think otherwise is all but heresy. But if educational leaders were to have a shift in thinking and focus on teachers first, think how much it could affect teacher job satisfaction, motivation, and performance.

Take for example, Vineet Nayar, CEO of Sampark and former CEO of HCL Technologies (one of the largest IT outsourcing companies in the world, who authored the book, *Employees First, Customers Second*). In the book (2010), he shares how he took over the control of HCL Technologies which had been a high-performing company but had become stagnate over the course of several years. Nayar was determined to make it excellent again. So after much self-examination within the company and discussion with employees of the company around the globe, he realized that everything hinged mainly on two important questions. In a Forbes interview, Nayar shared some insight into the questions and how he realized the employee is more important to him than the customer.

The first question is "what is the core business of any corporation?" and the answer is to create different shared value for its customers. This is really the same goal of education, to create different shared value. We see this "different shared value" as personalized education. Each student has different learning styles, needs, interests and passions. So the more we can offer our learners in regards to personalization, the better the outcome (societal outcome).

The second question is "where does that different shared value get created?" and the answer is in the interface of the employees and the customers. Hence, we ask if the employees in that interface create a different shared value, what should the business of managers and management be? The answer to that question is the business of managers and management should be to enthuse and encourage employees so that they can create a different shared value: enhance employees first and customers second. Here again in education, the interface is between the teacher and the student, then what is the function of the administration? It is to encourage and enthuse the teachers so they can create such experiences with the students.

Nayar believed that his managers had to encourage and serve these value-zone employees, rather than having the workers serve their managers. He believed that the company needed to put its employees first in order to achieve more effective customer service. Concentrating on your staff members and how they can contribute to your business is the best method for ensuring continued success. As effective administrators and educational leaders, the method to ensure maximized success in the classroom is to focus on teachers and they will take care of the students.

The question you may be asking yourself is if job satisfaction is even an issue among teachers. Well, unfortunately, according to the 2012 MetLife Teacher Survey, teacher satisfaction has declined 23 percentage points since 2008, from 62% to 39% very satisfied and the percentages are currently at the lowest level in 25 years. This reflects our own survey (which included hundreds of K–12 teachers from around the country) where 32% of participants said they were very satisfied with their teaching job (conducted via online survey 2017). A question similar to the satisfaction question asked participants to rate the morale of teachers in their schools and only 10% responded very high. Sixty-one percent of respondents rated morale as three or lower on a linear scale with five being very high and one being very low. Interestingly, nearly 70% of respondents believed that increasing teacher recognition would improve morale of teachers in the school.

Improving teacher job satisfaction is important because research showed that younger teachers are more likely to leave their jobs because of low job satisfaction, which leads to a shortage of teachers (Green-Reese, Johnson, & Campbell, 1991).

Yet, when teachers feel a high level of job satisfaction, they provided higher quality teaching and their students were more successful (Demirtas, 2010), which meant high teacher job satisfaction benefits education overall. In order to improve the quality of teaching and ease the difficulty of a shortage of teachers, it is very important to maintain teachers' high job satisfaction. The issue isn't just a teacher shortage, but high turnover rates as well.

Education is as much about the people as it is the policies and programs. We are aware that the relationship between a teacher and student is a critical part of a student's success in the classroom. But did you know that the relationship between administration and teachers is just as important for a positive school culture and success of students? Two of the most important factors in job satisfaction are the way that principals manage their schools and the relationships with faculty (Minarik, Thornton, & Perreault, 2003).

Increasing Satisfaction: The Survey Says . . .

As you can see from the different examples above, there are many factors which affect teacher job satisfaction. There are some factors, like pay and funds for resources, that administration may have limited or no control over in your position. These still affect job satisfaction so they should not be ignored, and we should do a better job of voicing our concerns on these matters as a society. However, there are many factors in which administration does have control.

As mentioned above, **the most important factor in job satisfaction tends to be the relationship between administration and**

faculty. Interestingly, this is a similar finding to the relationship between teacher and student affecting student success. Kathy Cox, former State Superintendent of Georgia, conducted a longitudinal study in schools across Georgia to see what factors most influenced student success (Johnson & McElroy, 2010). It turns out that factors such as parental involvement, socio economic status, etc., were important, but the most important factor was the relationship between student and teacher. So, it only makes sense that the most important factor for teacher job satisfaction is the relationship between teacher and administration. Within this relationship dynamic there has to be a level of respect, recognition, and responsibility, in essence treating teachers like professionals for them to experience a high level of job satisfaction.

This sentiment was echoed in our survey. The following are some of the responses to the question how can job satisfaction can be improved.

- Less testing pressure on our students. Also more things keep being added to Teachers' plates without taking anything away.
- Feel like I'm part of decisions that affect me and my students.
- If all members of my grade level team were willing to do their share.
- Working for administrators who appreciate the effort that teachers put in and that have the respect to acknowledge the staff.
- More reinforcement from administration that we are making a difference. More positive encounters from others—positive notes, messages, recognition throughout the year that don't feel forced (spur of the moment).
- Be present, and be consistent. Less of the "other" stuff. Meetings, paperwork, redundant emails.
- Let us have a strong voice at the district level. We know what is best for our kids.
- Administration that works with me, and not against me. They say they do what they do for the kids, but what about the teachers. I want to have a life outside of teaching.

- ◆ More planning time, more time, less new initiatives and more time to perfect the initiatives just implemented. We should not spend our weekends planning. We need time to be "human."
- ◆ Being respected for my experience. Not treating me like I need to be "trained" by people that aren't even in the classroom. Trust that I know what's "best for kids."
- ◆ Support from administration, positivity, encouragement.
- ◆ Feel that my thoughts and opinions are heard and matter.
- ◆ Being appreciated and recognized. If this does not come from parents—it needs to come from administration. Teachers are, in general, highly self-critical and reflective. They often don't need to be told what they need to do better. Build efficacy by believing in your staff.

As stated before, there were an abundance of responses related to increased pay, more resources available, more personalized professional development, and other factors that you may not be able to change or affect directly, but they are issues that shouldn't be ignored as well. There just needs to be a more organized and concerted effort for some of these changes to occur. However, most of the examples listed previously from the survey reflect factors that can be addressed by educational leaders in the schools or at the district level. One important point to note is that **"Most teachers don't quit their job, they quit their administration."** Regardless of pay and working conditions, most teachers stay or leave based upon the administration and the relationship they have with them. A teacher may say she is leaving because she will make a couple of thousand dollars more at a different school, but the reality is she is more than likely leaving because of the poor relationship with her administrators. If you want great teachers to stay, create a culture where they want to stay.

The Finnish Line

Before we leave the discussion of professionalism and job satisfaction, it is important to look at teaching in a country where teaching is highly respected and seen as a profession on the level of medical doctors. Finland has been a top performer on the PISA testing for several years. While there are many factors that may influence the scores, such as a more homogenous student population than here in the US, there is something to the level of autonomy and professionalism given to teachers that is noteworthy.

First of all, all teachers have to hold a master's degree and getting into the teaching programs are highly competitive since it is a well-respected profession. During their fifth year, teachers are placed into training schools, much like teaching hospitals at universities for medical students here in the US. During their internship, they are given the autonomy and flexibility to try out the theories they have learned at the university to which the school is affiliated. They are not given a curriculum and forced to follow it.

In an interview with the Guardian newspaper, Leena Krokfors, professor of teaching at Helsinki University, explains, "The high-level training is the basis for giving young teachers a great deal of autonomy to choose what methods they use in the classroom"—in contrast to England, Krokfors says, where she feels teaching is "somewhere between administration and giving tests to students" (Crouch, 2015). In Finland, teachers are largely free from external requirements such as inspection, standardized testing and government control; school inspections were scrapped in the 1990s (Crouch, 2015).

> Teachers need to have this high-quality education so they really do know how to use the freedom they are given, and learn to solve problems in a research-based way," Krokfors says. "The most important thing we teach them is to take pedagogical decisions and judgments for themselves.
>
> (Crouch, 2015)

So, while teachers are well trained in Finland, the biggest difference between the US and Finland is the autonomy and flexibility for teachers to be the experts in the classroom. Teachers are not micromanaged by administrators either. In the

TALIS (Teaching and Learning International Survey) which was compiled from several countries, there are three stats which stand out:

♦ There is no national framework for teacher appraisal in Finland. Thus, about one in four teachers in Finland (nearly 28%) works in a school where the principal reports that teachers are not formally appraised by the principal, well above the TALIS average of 14%. Instead, the main form of appraisal occurs through face-to-face and often informal dialogue with the school leader.
♦ Nearly 60% of teachers in Finland feel that their profession is valued in society, which is well above the average of 31% in TALIS countries.
♦ 91% of teachers in Finland are satisfied with their jobs (TALIS, 2013).

Five teachers of the year from the US visited Finland to see what they do differently. Their take away was not that they have a better curriculum or better programs in place, but that teachers are respected and given the autonomy to do what they do best, which is to teach in an innovative environment. We mentioned earlier that Finland has a more homogenous group of students than here in the US, so you may think a common curriculum would be even more beneficial. However, they score high on PISA, not because of a common curriculum, standardized testing, or even government incentives, but because they allow their teachers to be the leaders, experts, and innovators in the classroom. Finnish teachers are treated as professionals and given the freedom (autonomy) to teach as experts, which translates to high job satisfaction. Finland in essence has a "Teachers First" mindset, and this mindset permeates the schools and reflects on International Testing.

Ironically, Finnish educator Pasi Sahlberg, author of *Finnish Lessons*, was asked in an interview with *The Washington Post*, if Finnish teachers would perform better in the US with our standardized focused educational system. He replied,

I argue that if there were any gains in student achievement they would be marginal. Why? Education policies in Indiana and many other states in the United States create a context for teaching that limits (Finnish) teachers to use their skills, wisdom, and shared knowledge for the good of their students' learning. Actually, I have met some experienced Finnish-trained teachers in the United States who confirm this hypothesis. Based on what I have heard from them, it is also probable that many of those transported Finnish teachers would be already doing something else than teach by the end of their fifth year—quite like their American peers.

Conversely, the teachers from Indiana working in Finland—assuming they showed up fluent in Finnish—stand to flourish on account of the freedom to teach without the constraints of standardized curricula and the pressure of standardized testing; strong leadership from principals who know the classroom from years of experience as teachers; a professional culture of collaboration.

(Strauss, 2013)

At the end of the day teaching is a profession that should be held in high esteem. Teachers want to be respected, valued, and given the freedom to be the experts in the classroom. One of the reasons teachers are more highly regarded in some countries, like Finland, is that they are treated not just like adults, but as highly trained professionals by their administration. You are the one that can initiate the change in perception more than anyone else. In the next chapters, we'll look at how to do so.

2

Motivating Your
Teachers to Succeed

Walt Disney is one of the most recognized names in the world. His name has been synonymous with pop culture and entertainment for nearly a century. Walt Disney is also considered one of the great innovators in history. But what you may not know is that Walt was never an exemplary student. In fact, he only attended secondary school for one year. But there was one teacher who influenced his life so profoundly that they remained in touch throughout his adulthood. In an interview with the *Journal of the California Teachers Association* in 1955, Walt Disney shared his story of the teacher who encouraged and motivated him to follow his dreams (Barrier, 2007).

> The teacher I remember best, with affectionate respect, is Miss Daisy A. Beck. She taught the seventh grade in the old Benton Grammar School in Kansas City, Mo. She gave me the first inkling that learning could be enjoyable—even schoolbook learning. And that is a great moment in a kid's life. She had the knack of making things I had thought dull and useless seem interesting and exciting. I never forgot that lesson.

It was always my inclination to think in pictures rather than words. I was already dreaming of becoming an artist-a newspaper cartoonist, at this point. I spent many study hours drawing flipover figures on textbook margins-like the McGuffey readers-to entertain classmates.

Miss Beck understood this, too. She was not only tolerant about these extra-curricular activities, but actually encouraged them. She saw what she regarded as potential talents in other kids, too, and did everything she could to bring them out.

The point is, she tried to understand all of us as individuals. She managed somehow to promote our personal inclinations without neglecting the formal grade requirements.

Walt Disney is describing a teacher who was innovative in her teaching. She knew that students tend to be more focused and curious about things they do well or about which they are passionate. She helped students identify their strengths/talents and created an environment where they could develop them within the confines of the curriculum.

Because of the influence of a motivated teacher, Walt Disney later became one of the greatest innovative and creative entrepreneurs in history. He was not only innovative, but a great motivator in his own right. While his work with technology was innovative, he realized that his employees weren't properly equipped coming out of school. So, he actually set up his own art school for his employees when the traditional art schools were not offering what he wanted and needed to carry out his mission, since these schools were not always up to date with the latest technologies. When preparing to make Snow White, Walt sent his animators to classes in acting, fine arts, and even to classes on motion and gravity to ensure they had the training and materials to do their best.

When Disney presented a new idea to his staff, he would gather everyone in the studio, then act out the entire movie alone to personally show what he envisioned the story to be and give his artists direction. He brought the story to life and in doing so, sparked creativity and endless motivation for his employees. Imagine if you, as an administrator, created an environment of energy and enthusiasm within your faculty on a daily basis. How would that impact your school culture?

Think of how different our pop culture would be if it weren't for Walt Disney. There would not be the movies that we all grew up watching like *Snow White, Sleeping Beauty, Bambi,* and even *Pinocchio*. And no Mickey Mouse or Walt Disney World, which is the most visited theme park in the world. Although it wasn't all fame and success for Disney, he didn't let failure impede his motivation. In fact, experts have estimated that Walt Disney endured over 300 failures in his pursuit to create! But his motivation never wavered and he transformed pop culture with innovation and the Magic of Disney.

Nowhere should innovation and curiosity be more present than in education. With our focus on covering curriculum and preparing for standardized tests, we too often forget that teachers need freedom and autonomy to be the expert in the classroom. To energize their students and create that spark of creativity and curiosity that makes learning come alive!

Why Motivation Matters

Motivation has been a topic of discussion and research in the corporate world for decades. Gallup has done extensive research on the topic and their results show that people who are motivated, feel valued, and recognized, are six times more productive than people who don't feel this way (Flade, Asplund, & Elliot, 2015). Could you imagine what your school might look like if all of your faculty and staff were six times more productive than the average staff? You read that correctly, six times more productive! Sadly, two-thirds of employees surveyed don't feel this way. Motivation and job satisfaction not only affect job performance, but home life as well. Employees with low job satisfaction feel like it affects their personal lives as well and they feel like they have a lower quality of life. The reason may be that we equate so much of our self-worth, happiness, and even quality of life to our jobs. In fact, there is a large body of research that a loss of a job is about the same as a loss of a family member. So, if we aren't happy, satisfied, and motivated in a job, it's easy to see how it can negatively affect every area of our lives. If you want to see if your faculty is highly motivated, then see how curious and innovative they are. If they take risks, try new things, and open new doors, then they are motivated. Unmotivated teachers go through the motions, check off the boxes, and do what they're told simply because they have been conditioned to do so. Teachers should not be checking off the boxes, they should be thinking outside of them.

So, when we use the term "Teachers First," it's not just a catchy phrase, but there is a purpose to putting teachers first. Changing how teachers are viewed and how we support them is innovative in itself. After all, teacher motivation is critical to the growth and success of the educational system. Motivated Teachers are change agents who seek to innovate, inspire, and bring out the best in all students. **Motivated teachers inspire and motivate students!**

A recent Gallup poll of 170,000 Americans (10,000 of whom were teachers), found, "Of all the professions we studied in the U.S., teachers are the least likely to say that their opinions count and the least likely to say that their supervisor creates an open and sharing environment" (www.kqed.org/mindshift/ 36924/what-motivates-teachers). How can teachers be motivated and innovative in this type of environment? This is a troubling trend at a time when schools need to attract high-quality educators.

> If the perception in our country is that teaching is not a great profession to go into, we certainly aren't going to be encouraging really talented young people to be thinking about the profession of teaching or getting the most out the great teachers we already have in the classrooms.
>
> (Swartz, 2014)

Furthermore, according to sociologists, "current school environments are a reward-scarce setting for professional work and often seem to work against teachers' best efforts to grow professionally and improve student learning" (Peterson, 1995, 11).

Motivational Factors

Motivation is the internal and external factors that stimulate desire and energy in people to be continually interested and committed to a job, role, or subject, or to make an effort to attain a goal. Motivation results from the interaction of both conscious and unconscious factors such as the (1) intensity of desire or need, (2) incentive or reward value of the goal, and (3) expectations of the individual of her peers. Teachers who are motivated do what they need to do, when they need to do it. They may even go above and beyond depending on the source of the motivation.

Extrinsic factors refer to behavior that is driven by external rewards such as money, incentives, or even praise. However, in reality, extrinsic motivators are those factors that meet baseline needs of performing the job. Extrinsic factors stem from the work environment and are applied by someone other than the person being motivated. These extrinsic factors can include class size, discipline conditions, and availability of teaching materials. It can also include the quality of the principal's supervision and basic psychological needs such as money, status, and security. Based upon our surveys and research in the field, we have identified the following factors that are extrinsic motivation for our teachers:

- ◆ Compensation/incentives
- ◆ Resources/materials
- ◆ Leadership

In adequate supply, these factors don't necessarily increase motivation but they do prevent dissatisfaction. For example, while pay may not be a major motivator, even the most intrinsically motivated teacher will become discouraged if their salary doesn't pay the mortgage.

Compensation

We have heard teachers through the ages say that they didn't get into teaching for the money, but the lack of it can cause a great deal of dissatisfaction in the classroom. While you may have very little control over the salary of your teachers, it is important to be aware of the various situations in which your faculty may be. An important point to consider is that a new teacher with large debt, such as student loans, will view salary as more of a motivator than someone who has less student loan debt, or is at the higher end of the pay scale for degrees or experience.

The online education source, Chalkbeat, discussed this issue of compensation with educators in Colorado in article entitled, *Teacher by day, waitress by night: Colorado teachers work second jobs to make ends meet*. The article focused on one kindergarten teacher who works two extra jobs, as an event planner, and at a local gym just to make ends meet. She explained that the second and third jobs are a necessity—covering groceries, her gym membership, and helping repay the $20,000 loan she took out last year to make ends meet during her unpaid teaching internship.

The article also referenced a male teacher in Jefferson County, Colorado, a father of three who works as a bike mechanic and property manager on the side. He joked that he drinks ten cups of coffee a day just to have the energy to do it all. Sadly, 16% of teachers nationwide take on second jobs outside the school system, according to a 2014 report from the Center for American Progress. While the report only looked at data for one year, it does reflect a culture where our most important professionals have to take on extra jobs. The prevalence of teachers with second jobs is one symptom of larger, systemic problems—the steady erosion of teacher pay, constant school funding crunch, and no costs of living increases. But some teachers and outside observers say it's also a problem in its own right, depleting teachers' energy, diverting their focus from the classroom and contributing to decisions to leave the profession altogether for better paying careers. Regardless of your leadership positions, it is important for you to be an advocate for teacher pay and when you have the platform or opportunity to influence teacher pay, then be bold enough to speak up. Other ways to help teachers alleviate some of the stress of low pay, or extra work to make ends meet, is to get the community involved in giving back. Have businesses offer free spa days, or have businesses provide coffee on a regular basis for your faculty. These may not directly influence pay, but may help keep them motivated because they know you're doing what you can to help. In our survey, administrators shared the following ways they tried to increase compensation.

- ◆ Teachers receive stipends for earning extra certifications, outstanding assessment scores, etc.
- ◆ We reward for perfect teacher attendance and high scores on student surveys.
- ◆ We constantly push for competitive salaries in our district.
- ◆ We identify stipends or monetary awards from district or from community organizations.

Resources/Materials

You may recall the teacher peddler, Teresa Danks Roark, in Chapter 1 and the desire to have adequate resources for her class. According to research by (Gokce, 2010, 490), "teachers give importance to the needs that will increase their performance teaching-learning processes, but those needs are not in fact being adequately met." Teachers need materials and resources to adequately prepare for their lessons. In fact in our teacher survey, one of the most common responses was the need for adequate resources and materials for the classroom so teachers would not have to spend their own money.

Meredith Broussard discussed the lack of materials and resources in Philadelphia schools in her article, *Why Poor Schools*

Can't Win at Standardized Testing, which was featured in *The Atlantic* (Broussard, 2014). Ms. Broussard reported that Philadelphia teachers spend an average of $300–$1,000 of their own money each year to supplement their $100 annual budget for classroom supplies, according to a Philadelphia Federation of Teachers survey. Sometimes, they even resort to buying and using books and other materials that were used by another school, even if the books are not on the school's curriculum. After building a program to look at each Philadelphia public school to see whether the number of books at the school matched the number of students, Broussard found out that the average school only had 27% of the required books in the 2012–2013 year, and at least ten schools had no books at all. Some teachers hustle and negotiate to get books and paper and desks for their students. They spend their spare time running campaigns on fundraising sites like DonorsChoose.org, and they keep an eye out for any materials they can get from other schools.

This is not restricted to Philadelphia schools, but is a nation-wide problem. Teachers, even those on limited budgets, will spend their own money to ensure students have adequate resources, even teachers who work extra jobs. So, here again is an opportunity to reach out to the community for support if the funding is simply not there. Don't be afraid to launch your own online drives on sites such as GoFundMe, DonorsChoose, and Adopt-a-classroom. You can collect gift cards from businesses or even get the PTA involved with fundraisers. Even think outside the box and provide an annual auction, gala, or other opportunity for the school community to come together and raise money for the classrooms.

Leadership

While we have a whole section dedicated to leadership later in the book, it is important to include in this section since administrators can have a profound influence on the motivation of faculty.

Give Them Time and Space to Be Great

One of the main responses in our survey was teachers' lack of time to actually plan. Most teachers do need to adhere to a set curriculum most of the time, but giving them flexibility in planning and time to plan it can motivate them to be great. Did you know that in Finland, teachers teach about 4 hours per day? According to the OECD (Organization for Economic Cooperation and Development), an average Finnish teacher teaches 600 hours annually or about 4 or less lessons daily. An average US teacher spends almost double that time teaching with an average of over 1,080 hours of in-class instruction annually. This equals an average of six or more lessons per day. Also, teachers in Finland are not expected to be at school when they do not have a class. For example, if they don't have any afternoon classes on Thursdays, they can typically leave or if their first class on a Wednesday starts at 11:00, they don't have to be at school until that time. This system allows the Finnish teacher more time to plan and think about each lesson. It gives them time to be innovative.

Nurture Greatness

If anyone can appreciate a commitment to lifelong learning, it is a teacher. Teachers also understand that different learners have different needs, and the same is true of faculty as well. That is what makes ongoing professional development so valuable. By giving teachers new ways to reach more kids, you can remind them why they entered this field to begin with. Consider investing in seminars presenting new education technologies or pedagogical theories, like team building or project-based learning. Or maybe a topic that is of great interest to the teacher that can used in the classroom. Build on your teachers' strengths!

Respect Them

Teachers know that the language they use can nurture or interfere with their relationships with students. The same goes for administrators who want to connect with teachers. Use positive, respectful language at all times, and really listen to their concerns and observations. Remember teachers are professionals, not students, and they want to be treated as such. **Respect their time when it comes to meetings, committee, emails, paperwork, etc.** Ask yourself how important is this meeting, email, etc.? If it's not a priority, then don't make it one.

Challenge Them

Effective teachers want administrators to trust their experience, to give them more authority over their instruction, and to provide a fair measurement of how effectively they meet their students' needs—preferably without standardized testing being the only measurement. Remember back to your time in the classroom, how your students wanted to work hard for you and to make you proud? Well, your faculty want to do the same as well. But when they do go above and beyond, remember to recognize it; we are never too old to want to be recognized for a job well done.

Intrinsic Factors

What is motivating our teachers intrinsically?

- ◆ Autonomy/empowerment
- ◆ Mastery (Professional Development)
- ◆ Purpose

In his book, *Drive: The Surprising Truth About What Motivates Us*, author Daniel Pink describes three important factors for motivation in the workplace: autonomy, mastery, and purpose. These are three cornerstones of intrinsic motivation. Ironically, in a common core and standardized testing culture, these are precisely the factors that are being stripped away from teachers in the name of greater accountability.

Autonomy is our desire to be self-directed. It increases engagement over compliance. Effective teachers like to feel that they are seen as the experts. The way to make stars out of teachers is to let teachers be stars. Let them be an example of innovation, to let them find the path that works best for them and their students, even if sometimes this means failure. If they are allowed to search for the best methods or answers, guess what, they'll find them.

Autonomy can also be viewed as the freedom to develop collegial relationships among their peers to accomplish tasks. This means teachers don't necessarily see autonomy as walking into the classroom, closing the door, and doing whatever they want, but that it means they work with colleagues to create, develop, and implement strategies to improve teaching and learning. Collegiality can be expressed through experiencing challenging and stimulating work, creating school improvement plans, or even leading curriculum development. The literature suggests that collegiality is directly linked to effective schools (Johnson, 1986; Glatthorn & Fox, 1996), where "teachers valued and participated in norms of collegiality and continuous improvement (experimentation)" (Little, 1982, 1). While we will discuss collegiality and "teams" in a later section, it is important to note the importance of creating a collegial environment where teachers are motivated to work together.

Mastery is the desire to get better skills. In education, we refer to this as Professional Development (PD). Professional development can take on many forms. It can be a speaker, a mentor, a coach, an online course, or a myriad of other methods. Regardless of the type of PD presented, there are a few factors that need to be considered. These were the results of a survey by the Gates Education foundation (http://k12education. gatesfoundation.org/resource/teachers-know-best-teachers-views-on-professional-development/).

- ◆ **Relevance**. We always stress differentiation in the classroom, but don't follow this concept when it comes to training and development of teachers. So make sure the PD is relevant. As with students, teachers' professional learning needs are rarely one-size-fits-all. "It looks different in every context," one teacher told us. "It has to be personalized."
- ◆ **Interactive.** Rather than listening to lectures, teachers want to apply learning through demonstrations or modeling and practice. "The best usually involve hands-on strategies for the teacher to actually participate in," shared one teacher.

- ◆ **Delivered by someone who understands their experience.** Teachers value learning most when it comes from other teachers. "Anything that a fellow teacher who is still in the classroom [presents] beats out everything else," one educator said. We connect with people who have been "in the trenches" like we have and respond to them better.
- ◆ **Sustained over time.** Professional growth is a process, not an hour blocked off on a calendar. "PD needs to be something that you keep working on for a semester or a year," explained a teacher. The more personalized it is to the teachers, the more likely it is to be sustainable as well.
- ◆ **Treats teachers like professionals.** As one teacher told us, "PD should treat us as adults, rather than children." As obvious as this point is, it doesn't seem to be reflected in the reality of PD for most teachers—fewer than one in three are highly satisfied with current PD offerings.

Simply checking the boxes for PD is not satisfactory to effective teachers. They want meaningful and applicable training. Remember we are talking about educated people who desire to improve their mastery, so teachers want the best opportunities and training available.

Another way to motivate professional development is to arrange study groups (perhaps organized by grade level) to read a book or discuss and research a current hot topic. You can use this opportunity to read a book on education, leadership, relationships, or some other topic that can help improve the effectiveness of your teachers.

Finally, when we think of mentoring or coaching, we think either a new hire, or someone who may be struggling. So, there is often a negative connotation associated with mentoring or coaching. This should not be the case and in many instances, there should be more mentoring or coaching available. When new programs or curriculum are put in place, teachers prefer coaches who are subject-area experts trained in giving feedback and capable of sharing specific actions that can be tried in the classroom immediately. This is how mentoring and coaching should work. Many administrators don't have the time or sometimes specific expertise to be coaches, so here is an opportunity for a teacher to use her talents in coaching or developing PD that will benefit a teacher, team, or the whole faculty.

Purpose is the desire to do something that has meaning and is important. Businesses that only focus on profits without valuing purpose will end up with poor customer service and unhappy employees. Millennials, especially, are looking to work for organizations that have a clear sense of purpose. The Belgian beer brand Stella Artois is a great example of a company sharing a greater purpose. They have agreed to donate $ 4.8 million dollars over the next four years to the charity Water.org, which provides wells and fresh drinking water in needy countries around the world.

As we discussed in the opening section, many teachers do feel a "calling" or sense of purpose in teaching. And there is no greater sense of purpose in the professional world than educating and preparing our youth to be productive citizens. This doesn't mean that every day is going to be some epic event in the classroom. Somedays, life is just mundane and ordinary. But, teachers with a sense of purpose are able to see the big picture and can ride out the hard or boring days because their eye is on the bigger prize. That is where you as an administrator can make the difference in encouraging teachers, appreciating them, and celebrating even small successes on the road to the big things!

Innovation

Curiosity is the foundation of innovation. We open new doors and new ideas and keep moving forward. And it begins with administration. Are teachers motivated more by a leader who constantly tells them what to do or one who poses questions? Or better yet, allows them to pose questions? As we mentioned before, there is no other field where innovation and curiosity are more important than in education. We want students to develop a curiosity for learning and to develop their talents to be innovators who contribute to society. Well, the best way to get students curious and innovative is for teachers to reflect it. Teachers are more willing to exhibit these traits when they have administrators who encourage them to be innovative. In an interview with Brad Currie, he shares his thoughts on creating an environment of curiosity and innovation for his teachers. Mr. Currie currently serves as a Director of Planning, Research, and Evaluation for the Chester School District in Chester, New Jersey. He is the author of four books and he is part of the *ASCD Emerging Leaders Class of 2014*. Mr. Currie shared,

> Passionate educators should always look for ways to enhance their effectiveness and take risks. This only happens if they are part of an environment where they feel supported and can innovate in their own unique ways. I take great pride in finding new resources and methods to help my colleagues/faculty impact student success. One time, while sifting through some blog posts that my PLN posted on social media, I came across a website that Monica Burns featured on www.classtechtips.com. The tool provided opportunities for classrooms from around the world to connect with each other virtually. I thought that this would be a great way for our world language teachers to give their students a more in depth perspective on the cultures they are learning about in class. So, I emailed the link to our K–8 world language teachers and sure enough they were really interested in trying them out. Over the next few weeks and months, they were able to connect with and learn from various classrooms from around the world.
>
> Motivating staff comes in many shapes and sizes. Often, the most simple and effective ways are overlooked. I truly believe in the power of finding new methods and resources, exposing staff to these best practices, and giving them the green light to try it out in their educationsl spaces. Students take risks when they see teachers take risk. Teachers take risks when they see school and district leaders take risks. Supported risk-taking helps contribute

to a healthy school environment. It's what motivates and keeps educators passionate about the important work they do on a daily basis.

Some administrators shy away from innovative or outside the box thinking. Mainly because it doesn't fit into the scheme of neatly packaged curriculum. While innovative thinking can be a little messy at times, it does reflect the real world. The classroom, after all, should look more like a construction site than a museum. Innovation sometimes comes with its share of risks and failures. The CEO of Paypal, Dan Schulman, shared in a television interview that he sought out people who had failed and failed miserably. He said he knew these people were innovators. People who are curious and look for new ideas or ways to do things. He said that we forget that innovation has a fairly high failure rate. However, it's not the failures that matter, but what you do with them. . . . How you grow from them and move forward. Don't ever stifle people who are willing to take risks.

In his book *Great by Choice*, Jim Collins encourages organizations to shoot bullets first, then cannonballs. His point is that while we need to take risks, we need to make sure the risks we take are calculated ones. In his organization he said,

> We've tried a lot of different things over the years. Some worked and others haven't. But even the failures can lead to future successes . . . because we learn from them and enter into the risks with appropriate research and caution.
>
> (Collins, 2011)

So, innovation is about taking these calculated risks and not being afraid to fail. We want students to have the confidence to take risks and be curious and innovative. But, how can they if teachers aren't motivated to try new and creative ways of reaching the students? Is your school culture a catalyst for innovation? It's important to listen to your teachers, listen to their ideas, and build a space of trust and openness that allows everyone to feel comfortable and encouraged to come forward with new ideas. Ultimately, it is about building **trust** in your staff to take risks in a safe environment. That's when, in the manner of Walt Disney himself, magic is created!

Chapter 2: Key Points to Remember

Teachers who are motivated do what they need to do, when they need to do it. If they feel supported and encouraged to try new things, they will even go above and beyond. Remember: motivated teachers are more engaged, more productive, and have a more positive outlook. Motivated teachers lead to better students. Keep in mind these strategies and begin motivating your teachers today!

- ◆ **Recognize them.** A teacher's greatest desire, after student success, may be to receive respect and recognition from the administration. Remember, the administration is the key factor in whether or not a teacher leaves. Don't give the good teachers a reason to leave.
- ◆ **Respect.** Respect is a great motivator, especially when it seems teachers get very little. Don't just show them respect in your collegiality, but respect their time when it comes to meetings, emails, workload, etc.
- ◆ **Allow more collaboration.** Teachers are lifelong learners. That means they are constantly trying to grow and flourish. A key way to fuel teacher motivation is to provide opportunities to collaborate. This doesn't mean more meetings, but actual time to plan with their colleagues.
- ◆ **Innovation.** Allow teachers the opportunity to try new things, even if they fail. Innovation is what brings about advances, improvements, and new creations (remember our Walt Disney story). Lack of innovation is one reason why teachers feel like their strengths are not being utilized, but feel like they are simply following a prepackaged curriculum.

◆ **Twitter PLNs.** Just as Mr. Currie took to Twitter to find interesting opportunities for his faculty, make sure to encourage your teachers to do the same. PLN (Professional learning networks) on Twitter and other social media are great resources for new and creative ideas!

3

Creating a Culture of Appreciation

Sargent Shriver made a startling statement during the speech he delivered on October 13, 1972, as part of his vice presidential campaign with George McGovern. He said that teaching was the hardest job in America.

As Sargent explained,

- ♦ It's not just "because the teachers of America have been blamed and castigated for all the ills of our educational system [. . .]
- ♦ not just because government refuses to recognize what inflation has done to teachers' salaries—and makes them scape goats for inadequate and short-sighted school budgets [. . .]
- ♦ not just because teachers often work in archaic schools with inadequate facilities for both teacher and child [. . .]
- ♦ not just because a narrow officialdom has bogged teachers down in massive red tape wasteful of time and destructive of initiative.

(Taken from the argent Shriver archives @ sargentshriver.org/ speech-article/the-hardest-job-in-america)

Sadly, 45 years later, there is still some truth to these statements. Teaching is still the hardest job in America. We seem to add more to teachers' plates instead of making things better for them. And it's not just the hardest job in America, but probably the least appreciated one, too. We have already discussed how it's not viewed as a profession, and in many cases, it's associated with being a glorified babysitter. Just about every politician runs on a platform of "fixing education." Every teacher has heard the, "you have summers off" decree about why the job must be easy. But the reality is that teaching is a hard job and it is greatly undervalued in our culture. And sometimes that mentality makes its way into the school building itself. We need to show our support by creating a culture of appreciation and putting teachers first!

Interestingly, when talking with corporate leaders, they often say they prefer to hire teachers because they possess good leadership, communication, and presentation skills (Johnson & Sessions, 2016). And in a culture where education is viewed as failing, let's not forget that it is in fact **teachers who make education successful at all**. Teachers spend countless hours of their own time to prepare lessons and grade work. They spend their own money on supplies. They spend their summers reading and learning how to do their jobs better. And they often become emotionally invested in the well-being of their students. So, let's not take for granted the superstars who step in the trenches on a daily basis to inspire and develop the next generation.

Teacher Appreciation Week Isn't Enough

While it is great that we set aside a week every May for Teacher Appreciation (www.pta.org/home/events/PTA-Teacher-Appreciation-Week), it's important to make appreciation go further than a thank you. As we have discussed, teachers are generally undervalued and under-appreciated in our society. **Appreciation is not just a pat on the back, but an ability to understand the worth, quality, or importance of something**.

It is, in essence, the ability to recognize someone's good qualities. A culture of appreciation builds on this recognition with a focus on instilling trust, teamwork, and a respect for the individual contributions of the classroom teacher.

Why is appreciation so important? Let's turn to Chester Elton for some facts and figures. Elton, an international speaker and NY Times bestselling author of *The Carrot Principle*, is affectionately known as the Apostle of Appreciation. He explains that "appreciation is really about recognizing the value of your employees." (Elton, 2009, 14) In his book, he shares some eye-opening statistics related to employee appreciation.

- ◆ Only 26% of employers show recognition and appreciation of employees on a regular basis. Of the 74% who do not, the reasons range from fear of what their management will think to management who thinks it is a waste of time.
- ◆ Of employees surveyed with highest morale, 94% believe their managers are effective at recognition, while 56% of employees with low morale give their managers a failing grade on recognition.
- ◆ 79% of employees who quit their jobs cite a lack of appreciation as a key reason for quitting.
- ◆ Two of the top four responses to "what do you really want from your job?" included recognition, and better relationships with their manager.

(Elton, 2009, 3–9)

As Elton explains, everyone needs to be appreciated and everyone likes to be recognized for a job well done. Elton shares an experience of visiting a Hard Rock Café to see how employees were engaged in their jobs. He said he walked into one particular Hard Rock, where the dishwasher was jamming out to music while he washed dishes. Elton observed that when a manager has created a culture where even the dishwasher is happy, then you know you're doing things right. As he says, "If the dish washer is happy, then everyone is happy." (From direct interview with Chester Elton) So, when you think about appreciation, think about not only teachers but your entire staff, and create a true culture of appreciation throughout the building. For example, do the custodians and bus drivers feel appreciated? What about the lunchroom workers or even the office staff? When people visit your schools, they can get a sense of your leadership by how the staff and teachers greet and interact with them. And as we will see in this section, having a culture of appreciation is a two-way street, where you will end up being more appreciated for your own effort as well.

Appreciation in Action: One Principal's Story

Mitch Young is a principal at a top performing high school in Georgia. In an interview, he shared his experiences improving a school that had a bad reputation, that parents didn't want their children to attend. There was school choice in that county of Georgia, and when he first arrived, there were a lot more requests to transfer from the school than to transfer into the school. So his goal was to change the perception of the school by starting with the teachers. As he shared, "I tried to 'empower' my teachers at greater levels to make decisions and to be 'encouraged' to share their expertise. In the end, I believe they appreciate the professional trust I have with them" (Young, 2017, direct interview with Mitch Young). He got input from them on a variety of topics, such as on how to revamp the way they marketed their STEM Academy in order to get more students in.

> We celebrated, publicly, our achievement of the recognition of becoming a Georgia-certified STEM program. Students had always been allowed to come, but with better marketing by not only teachers, but kids in the program, we now have a lot more coming in from around the county.
> (Young, 2017, direct interview with Mitch Young)

While he made many changes with faculty input, he thinks there are three things that made the biggest impact:

◆ *Bringing community members into the classroom, and teachers into the community:* First, he wanted to showcase his faculty to the community, so he could change the perception of the school. So he had business and community leaders visit the school on a regular basis to see his superstars in action. They would visit classrooms, sit in on lessons, and then engage with teachers between classes. Business leaders, who originally came just to see the STEM Academy, were brought into classes *throughout* the school. This had a great impact on non-STEM teachers feeling encouraged and appreciated. Then, to further improve this relationship and help teachers connect their classes to the real world, Mitch would take his teachers on a "field trip" to the businesses to see exactly what skills and knowledge students needed to work in these particular businesses. These businesses included technology, graphic design, and even a manufacturing company that makes the instant lotto tickets for the state's lottery. After meeting with HR, engineers, managers, production workers, and many other positions, the teachers gained a sense of what is needed by their students in the real world.

♦ *Encouraging teachers to do branding through social media:* Mitch says he believes his teachers are the best branding and advertising for his school. He encourages his teachers to develop webpages, social media accounts, and other means by which to show their students work and to connect with the community. While some administrators are still reserved about social media and especially interaction between faculty and students, Mitch believes it is simply a means for showing off the school.

♦ *Having teachers speak at meetings and conferences:* Finally, he shows his appreciation for his teachers by using their talents and expertise in community meetings and conferences. He uses every opportunity to have his teachers speak to a civic group, business luncheon, or other organizations. In addition, he encourages them to speak at conferences if they are willing. If some teachers are hesitant about speaking in front of large groups or groups of unfamiliar people, he will encourage them to share to small groups or even colleagues because he knows they have expertise to share.

Mitch shared that over the past three years since making those changes, the number of requests to come into his school are much greater than the requests to transfer. He also noted that his school has now been voted the best school in the county for three years in a row. The lesson we can take away is that your teachers can be one of your greatest assets if they are publicly recognized, involved, and appreciated through different means.

A Closer Look at Why We Need to Recognize Teachers

We looked at Chester Elton's observations on appreciation and Mitch Young's success story. But here are some additional statistics on why we need a culture of appreciation. Gallup asked more than 25 million employees around the world—including more than 100,000 educators—about what makes them engaged at work (www.gallup.com/services/178709/state-america-schools-report.aspx). K–12 teachers rate one item lower than any other on the survey: "In the last seven days, I have received recognition or praise for doing good work." Just 29% of teachers in Gallup's survey say they "strongly agree" with this statement. Yes, you read it correctly, only 29% strongly agreed with that statement.

Being recognized not only makes teachers feel good; it also improves their perception of you as a leader. In the survey, Gallup asked teachers to rate their principal on a wide range of measures including management style, philosophy, and school climate. Principals with the highest level of talent elicited an interesting set of responses from their teachers. These effective principals:

- ◆ value recognition as a frequent and ongoing activity that builds a strong, positive school culture
- ◆ see recognition as a necessary ingredient and key driver of school success, rather than just another event on their calendar

◆ take the lead and get personally involved by playing an active role in the recognition process

◆ are not content with being the sole source of recognition, and build an environment in which recognition is contagious and everyone plays an important role.

As the research shows, the current culture needs to change. By creating a new culture of appreciation, you not only positively impact your faculty, but you will also be viewed much more positively by your faculty. It's a win-win!

How to Show Appreciation More Regularly

Appreciation is shown through building a relationship based on trust, respect, and open communication. Think about it—if you appreciate someone in your personal life, such as a spouse, you don't just show it once. You show it consistently. The same is true of appreciating your teachers. It's not a one-time deal but something you do on a consistent basis. Appreciation is about valuing your faculty, and it is an expression of admiration or gratitude. **Appreciation is not something you say, but something you show.** The following strategies reflect the feedback from our survey. The most common responses by teachers on how administrators could show more appreciation included:

◆ Be clear and consistent. Admit mistakes.
◆ Value communication. Listen to us. Have our voices heard.
◆ Actually take time to listen. Build relationships.
◆ Be more visible. More classroom walkthroughs/visits.
◆ Be supportive of all teachers, not just favorites.
◆ Involve us more in decision-making. Respect us and our opinions.
◆ Stop adding more to our plate and more acknowledgement of what we already do.

The responses can be categorized into two themes: relationships and character traits (respect and trust). This is because appreciation is as much about *connecting* with your teachers as it is about anything else. Here are a few strategies, aligned with the survey responses, to help you start building a culture of appreciation for your teachers and your whole staff. While some of these strategies will be discussed in more detail in later chapters, it is important to connect them with appreciation and recognition here as well.

Strategies for Building Relationships

Relationships are the foundation for building this new culture. If there is one thing we know for sure, it's that the relationship between a teacher and student is key to student success. But the same is true of the administrator and teacher relationship. So, I don't mean you should develop a surface-level friendliness among your faculty. True relationships are built upon deep trust that allows for the healthy expression of ideas and conflict without fear of repercussion. Your faculty need to know that you see them as people first and employees second. The old adage, "students don't care how much you know until they know how much you care" is true outside the classroom as well. Relationships trump everything else. It is in building these relationships that we learn to trust, respect, and even appreciate each other. I will discuss the importance of having high EQ as an administrator in a later section, but it is important to note here that if you aren't known to have the best interpersonal skills, then these strategies will be a roadmap for increasing your relationship with your faculty. Here are just a few ways to show appreciation while building a positive, deeper relationship with your faculty.

- *Remain visible* and approachable through the school day. The principal should NOT be hard to find. Instead of being tucked away in the office, be out in the classrooms. Be in the hallways to greet teachers and students to start each day. This may seem like it is not a good use of time, but it is more important than you realize.
- *Attend events* such as marriages or funerals of staff members' loved ones. The respective staff members will never

forget your thoughtfulness! Also, teachers appreciate when the principal calls to check on them if they have missed a couple of days of school due to illness. My brother is a sheriff in Georgia. One of his goals is to attend as many funerals in the county as possible, not just for family of his staff, but for as many citizens as possible. This does take up some of his free time. But as he says, "as the most visible elected official in the county, I feel like it is my responsibility to be there for the citizens of the county. You have no idea how much the families appreciate it when I make the effort to go by the funeral home. I feel it is part of my duty because I serve all the people of the county, and no better time to be there than during their time of need"(Direct interview with Jeff Johnson). So when you have the opportunity, make the effort to go the extra mile with your teachers and your entire school community. You may not realize just what it may mean to them as well.

◆ *Accommodate the personal needs of the staff.* Can you help cover a teacher's class when the teacher's child is performing in a play, receiving an award, etc.? Do you have a teacher who is working on an advanced degree, or traveling for a conference? Cover the last class of the day so the teacher can beat the traffic, or get the teacher a sub for half day so the teacher doesn't have to feel rushed the rest of the afternoon.

◆ *Be mindful of teacher workloads and stress levels.* If you notice that staff members are overwhelmed, take the time to ask what you can do to help or what resources can be shifted to help them execute their tasks. By noticing the pressure they're under and making a genuine effort to help, you'll not only ensure that tasks are completed in an effective and efficient manner, but you'll also create a necessary bridge to trust and appreciation from your employees.

◆ *Be sincere.* There is an old joke that says the key to any relationship is sincerity, and once you can fake that then you have it made. Well, do not fake sincerity. Be authentic and sincere in your motives, in your word, and in everything you do. Sincerity is about being genuine, honest, open, and truthful. Sincerity also involves showing that you genuinely believe in the school mission and the ability of your teachers. If you don't believe in what you are asking teachers to do, how will they believe in it either?

Pause to Reflect: What are two ways you can show teachers you appreciate them?

Strategies for Building Respect and Trust

The main character traits reflected in the survey were respect and trust. *Respect* defines the feeling of holding an entity or person in a high esteem, or valuing their opinions greatly. *Trust* means that a person places complete confidence in another person. Do you value your teachers and have full confidence in them? This means creating an environment where teachers feel safe to speak their mind, to discuss issues openly and with honesty, to take risks, and yes, even to fail. If teachers don't feel a high level of trust and respect for administrators, then they will never be fully committed to them or their vision. Teachers should feel comfortable when problems arise. Before teachers can rally around a solution, they often need to feel that their concerns have been heard and validated. Here are a few strategies to help improve the level of trust as it relates to teacher appreciation.

◆ *Improve communication.* Too often leaders are focused on an agenda and trying to reach goals without really listening to others. Teachers need to feel like they are heard. This means leaders show empathy and truly seek to understand the daily challenges and requests from teachers. As I heard Andy Stanley, pastor and bestselling author, share in a conversation once, "**Leaders who** refuse to listen will eventually be surrounded by people who have nothing significant to say." So make sure communication is not just you talking, but listening as well. And this doesn't just mean communicating about the business of the school, but the interests of your teachers as well. Get to know your faculty!

◆ *Keep promises.* Teachers want leaders who keep their word—who make commitments carefully but stick to them. Effective leaders make honesty and sincerity the foundation of their leadership. They seek to keep their promises at all costs. You have probably heard the saying, "It takes a lifetime to build a good reputation, but it can take just a second to destroy it." Be open and honest so your faculty can have confidence in your leadership. Part of this requires truthfulness, which means presenting the facts to the best of your knowledge. Being wrong is not the same thing as being dishonest.

◆ *Take responsibility for mistakes.* Even the most trustworthy leaders make mistakes. We are all human after all. The key is to quickly right the wrong and admit the mistake. Teachers respect leaders who own their mistakes and apologize immediately to those who were harmed. They do everything possible to avoid hurt feelings and bad blood. **Remember, even great leaders make mistakes, but they don't make excuses.** Be accountable to those you lead.

◆ *Be transparent and authentic.* Teachers want their leaders to be transparent and open. This means no hidden agendas. Authentic leaders reveal who they are and show what they value. They are self-aware and express their thoughts and feelings in healthy, caring ways. This also means having an open-door policy for teachers. However, being transparent doesn't mean you share everything, such as personal issues. Be careful not to reveal inappropriate personal details, talk about yourself incessantly, or tell people how you feel all the time. You should always ask yourself before a personal disclosure: is this relevant to the task or topic at hand?

◆ *Give teachers responsibility.* As administrators, you believe that teachers are leaders, but do you give them responsibility or authority outside of their classroom? There is nothing more frustrating or in conflict with appreciation than asking faculty to be part of a decision-making process, such as serving on a committee, and then disregarding their ideas or decisions. Don't add more responsibility to their plate without including real decision-making authority. If you ask people to serve in different capacities, trust them with authority and accountability. Also, be careful not to micromanage. Micromanaging is often due to a lack of trust, and it shows. Let your teachers know you trust them and believe in their abilities. Remember, as an administrator, your job is enormous, and it's difficult for you to excel in everything. If you are aware of your own strengths and weaknesses, you will have a clearer roadmap of where you need support. Teacher leaders can be the perfect complement if you let them. And they'll feel more appreciated as a result.

 Pause to Reflect: How can you build trust with your teachers?

Benefits of Appreciation

There would be no need to focus so much on teacher appreciation or recognition if there were no benefit to it. But as you might recall from the Carrot Principle research, nearly 80% of people who quit their jobs cite a lack of appreciation as a key reason for quitting. And of the people surveyed with highest morale, 94% believe their managers are effective at recognition and appreciation. The research is clear that appreciation has a profound effect on teachers and the school culture in general.

◆ *Appreciation makes people more engaged and productive at work, happy, and satisfied.* According to a survey by

GloboForce, a performance management company, there is a direct correlation between appreciation and happiness. Eighty-six percent of employees say they feel happier and prouder at work as a result of being recognized, while 85% say recognition made them feel more satisfied with their jobs (http://go.globoforce.com/rs/862-JIQ-698/images/ROIofRecognition.pdf). Imagine having teachers who are highly motivated, engaged, and full of energy. Imagine how that would affect learning in their classrooms.

◆ *Appreciation increases retention and makes teachers more likely to stay with their school.* While we discussed the reasons for people leaving teaching, the fact is that 40% to 50% of teachers leave the field within the first five years. Richard Ingersoll, who has studied the issue for years, says there's a revolving door of teacher turnover that costs school districts upwards of $2.2 billion a year nationally (Ingersoll, 2001). Yes, that's $2.2 billion with a B! Now imagine creating a culture where teachers are appreciated, where they want to stay and enjoy working. There would be less of a need for the expenses of new teacher induction and teacher mentoring. You would have a well-oiled Championship Team!

◆ *Appreciated teachers are more likely to receive higher satisfaction scores from students and parents.* One of the issues with teachers as professionals is the level of respect or lack thereof by the general population. But, what if students and parents viewed teachers in a much more positive light? In a study by Jacob and Lefgren, "parents strongly prefer teachers whom principals describe as the most popular with students—that is, those who are good at promoting student satisfaction. In contrast, parents place relatively less value on a teacher's ability to raise standardized mathematics or reading achievement scores. This suggests that "softer" teacher attributes may be quite important to parents" (2007, 1636). Students and parents generally want teachers who promote student satisfaction. Wouldn't it make sense that teachers who feel appreciated and have high job satisfaction would reflect this same attitude in the classroom? Imagine the positive image that your school could have in the community, just like Mitch Young has done with his school.

◆ *Appreciated teachers are more likely to trust their school leaders.* It is surprising how a little appreciation can go a long way to build trust. "In schools that are improving, where trust and cooperative adult efforts are strong, students report that they feel safe, sense that teachers care about them, and experience greater academic challenge. In contrast, in schools with flat or declining test scores, teachers are more likely to state that they do not trust one another" (Sebring & Bryk, 2000, 443). A culture of appreciation will build a level of trust that will transform your school.

Remember that when students succeed, it's not because of a curriculum or program, but because of great teachers. Imagine a school where teachers are happy, engaged, and actually want to stay. Imagine the teachers always feel appreciated and have the support to try new and innovative strategies. It all begins with the administration, who set the tone for the school culture!

Chapter 3: Key Points to Remember

Remember that everyone likes to feel appreciated. Appreciation shows that we value someone and that they have worth. But this does not just mean you say thank you or give a pat on the back. True appreciation is reflected in your relationships, in the responsibility you give others, and in the value you give their work. Teachers respond to appreciation because it confirms they matter and their work has value. When teachers and their work are valued, their satisfaction and productivity rises, and they are motivated to maintain or improve their good work. This is true of your whole staff because at the end of the day, regardless of their roles, we are all humans first. As we close this chapter, here are ways to take the lead in creating a culture of appreciation:

+ Be seen, especially in the classrooms. Great teachers like to be seen doing what they do best. This is a great way to stay connected to teachers and students!
+ Know your staff beyond the classroom. Engage with them outside of school as well. Even get them to share their expertise in the community.
+ Let teachers know you appreciate them. Send them personalized notes. One great idea is to begin each school year with a handwritten note for teachers waiting for them on their desk like the Apple note in the opening!
+ Be mindful of their full plates, especially at high stress times, such as during testing.
+ Remember it's all about developing positive relationships!
+ Understand that appreciation is a continual process. It should become a habit!

4

Learning to Become
a Selfless Leader

Effective leaders don't desire to lead, but rather desire to serve
—Brad Johnson

If teaching is the hardest job in America, then being an administrator, especially a principal, may be the toughest leadership job in America. According to *The Hechinger Report*, nearly 30% of principals who lead troubled schools quit every year, and by Year 3, more than half of all principals leave their jobs. The problem with this high rate of turnover is that principals leave before they are able to improve culture, motivation, morale, and school functioning.

How can you reverse this trend? One key way is to move from being a transactional leader to a servant leader who puts teachers first. To begin our discussion of what that means, let's step outside of education to look at a powerful example of selfless leadership. In 1997, the USS Benfold of the US Navy Pacific Fleet had a change in leadership. A new captain, Mike Abrashoff, whom I was fortunate enough to interview, was to take over as commander of the ship. His first experience was the reception aboard the ship to bid the former captain farewell. The crew seemed glad and relieved, almost celebratory, that the former captain was leaving. It turns out that the former captain was a very intelligent man, but he made the crew feel inferior and was condescending to them, which negatively affected the morale and culture of the ship. The ship's performance was ranked last in the fleet and the crew didn't feel safe should they be called into action.

Abrashoff recalled, "As I watched the ceremony that day and the reaction of the crew, I wondered to myself how the crew would react when I leave the ship after my tenure as captain?" He said this put things into perspective quickly for him. He knew his goal was to focus on improving the morale of the crew. He said,

> At this point in my career, other than sinking the ship, I knew I was set as far as retirement and even advancing in rank, so my goal wasn't to use the appointment to simply advance. Instead, I wanted to make a real difference in the crew of this ship.

Over the course of his tenure as captain, Abrashoff implemented many strategies that helped build a positive culture. For instance, he created an environment in which crew members felt safe to take risks and take ownership in the crew's success. As Abrashoff replied, "I took responsibility for the actions of the crew, so they knew I had their back, even if they failed." Captain Abrashoff would also publicly praise the crew when they did good work, in fact the crew affectionately named him "Mega Mike" because he would constantly praise his crew, which improved morale.

Sounding as much like a college coach as a ship captain, he said the reason that he felt like he needed to focus on the crew was that he wanted the parents of these young soldiers to be proud that their children were under his leadership. He didn't see them just as a crew; he got to know them personally and found out their interests and strengths, so he could best utilize their talents aboard the ship. Over the course of approximately two years, Abrashoff so profoundly changed the culture of the

USS Benfold that it went from being one of the worst perform-ing ships in the Navy to the best ship in the fleet.

Interestingly, as his time as captain came to an end, he decided that he didn't want the traditional pomp and circumstance given to such an occasion. Instead, he had 310 lobsters flown in for the last dinner with his crew. As he said, "I knew many of them had never seen, much less eaten a lobster." Then the next morn-ing, rather than the traditional ceremony, which he had experi-enced when coming on board, he simply gathered his crew around him on deck in their working coveralls, and gave what is known as the shortest change of command speech in military history. He simply told them, "You know how I feel." He said he left that day with pride, not so much for having made the ship the best in the Navy, but for having left an accomplished, tightknit, effective crew that he was unabashedly proud to have commanded (Johnson & Sessions, 2016, p. 54).

What can we learn from Captain Abrashoff? He didn't focus on transactional tasks such as policies, procedures, or trying to improve the ranking of the ship; he selflessly focused on building relationships and improving the morale of the crew. In turn, he, along with the crew, took one the lowest performing ships in the Navy and made it the highest performing ship in just two years. He made the turn-around with the same crew he inherited. But unlike his predecessors, he focused on building the strengths of his crew, raising morale, and giving them ownership in running the ship. In fact, the title of his bestselling book is, *It's Your Ship*!

The similarities between Captain Abrashoff and a school prin-cipal are quite striking. Both inherit a crew or faculty that already exists and has been influenced by the previous leader. They can make some changes, but for the most part, they have to lead the group that is already there. They also don't have a lot of time to make impactful changes. So it's key for them to focus not on programs or policies, but on the people who are there. Whether you are a new administrator or a seasoned veteran, you can cre-ate the same positive culture by focusing on the strengths of your teachers and giving them ownership of the school!

Leadership Styles

As a leader, focusing on your staff is key. But we should also take a moment here to point out that there is no perfect leader. That's right, there is no perfect leader. Hopefully that statement will help remove a burden you feel, one that has been imposed on you or possibly even self-imposed. You don't have to be perfect to be an effective leader. In fact, effective leadership is not about the leader at all, but it is about using your talents, abilities, and expertise to facilitate the success of others. Effective leadership is a selfless endeavor.

Top leaders in every field, including education, business, sports, and the military, often say that they see themselves as servant leaders (Johnson & Sessions, 2016). Some of you may be unfamiliar with this term, and in fact many leaders aren't aware of the differences among leadership styles or which style they use the most. The most common styles are transactional, trans-formational, situational, and servant leadership. The two we will examine are transactional leadership, which is the most common but least effective style, and servant leadership, which is considered the most effective.

While education has made an effort to adapt to 21st-century learning, leadership has remained relatively unchanged since the industrial revolution. In fact, most leadership, including educational leadership, was built upon the transactional (rewards versus punishment) leadership lens that was developed during the industrial revolution. **Transactional leadership** is a basic managerial style focused on controlling, organizing, and short-term planning. This doesn't mean that transactional leadership is necessarily bad, but that it is insufficient in maximizing the potential of the leader or the staff. Some of the key elements include:

- ◆ Based around power and position
- ◆ Focused on the short term, not on long-term success
- ◆ Behavioralist (rewards versus punishment)
- ◆ Efficiency-centered (bottom line-only focused)
- ◆ Structure-dependent (thinks inside the box) (Johnson & Sessions, 2016).

As you can see, a transactional style stifles some of the key elements in education, such as autonomy and innovation. If your leadership style is mostly transactional, you can see why it is difficult to give up some control and structure to allow your teachers to take ownership in the culture of the school. The fact that leadership has remained relatively unchanged, with predominantly transactional traits, could be a factor in why education is not as effective as it could be and is maybe even part of the issue with high turnover rate.

Servant leadership, on the other hand, may be less common, but it is in many respects the most effective and enduring style. This style doesn't mean that the leader acts as a servant to followers and has no leadership authority, but rather that the leader focuses on encouraging, empowering, and equipping followers to be successful. The focus is on the people. This style is often portrayed as an inverted pyramid where the followers, not the leaders, are on top. Some of the key elements of this style are shown in Table 4.1.

This style of leadership is most fulfilling to the leader and to the staff. However, one of the issues in education is that novice leaders aren't given much time to develop into this type of leaders. They are expected to produce certain results in a limited amount of time and if they don't, then someone else is placed in the position. The problem with this type of transactional

TABLE 4.1 Servant Leadership Attributes

Servant Leadership	
Traits	*Qualities*
◆ Listening	◆ Respect
◆ Empathy	◆ Responsibility
◆ Healing	◆ Humility
◆ Awareness	◆ Love
◆ Persuasion	◆ Compassion
◆ Conceptualization	◆ Commitment
◆ Foresight	◆ Patience
◆ Stewardship	
◆ Commitment to the growth of people	
◆ Building community	

leadership is that there are no long-term solutions implemented and there is little input from or focus on the teachers. So the vicious cycle continues, with administration turnover and little time spent on the teachers.

 Pause to Reflect: Do you think your leadership style is transactional, servant, or a mix? Explain.

The Selfless Leader

If servant leadership is ideal, then how can you learn to adapt that style? How can you create a culture where you are focused on your teachers and on empowering them to be their best? In reality, it can be hard to be so other-focused. We are by nature selfish, not selfless. And some leaders like the feeling of power and having their egos stroked. Selflessness is all about strength, and it's not for weak leaders. Weak leaders take the path of least resistance and that typically means being selfish, such as wanting all the credit and none of the blame. Real strength is measured by what we enable our followers to accomplish through our service to them, not by the pressure of the demands we place on them. Just as we tell teachers that the students come first, selfless leaders put their teachers first.

This is what separates great leaders from average leaders. As a selfless leader, you have to put your pride and ambition aside and focus more on the idea that you **"Bring your Assets, not your Agenda."** When we are promoted to leadership levels, there is the tendency to bring an agenda and make it about us. We desire to advance further, make more money, or get recognition for what we have accomplished. But when you bring your assets instead, your view changes considerably. For example, here's a story a friend shared about meeting a homeless person on a city street. When you meet this person, you don't have an agenda, because the person is in no position to help you. But, you do have your assets. Whether it is time, money, access to food, or clothing, you have the ability to impact this homeless person. Your focus is not on yourself, your position, or even how the situation can benefit you, but on helping the homeless person.

Now bring this mentality to your leadership position. Don't look at what is in it for you, or how you can benefit, but how can you help the people you lead. Your position, authority, and leadership skills are the assets you can use to help your teachers succeed. It's okay to be driven, to have goals, and desire to be even more successful, but as a leader, make your focus those you lead and how you can help them be even more successful. This is a great first step in becoming a selfless leader.

Becoming a Selfless Leader

When you become other-focused, then you can make positive changes to the school culture. Below are some of the key strategies that will help you move **from a desire to lead to a desire to serve**. These will increase your assets and value to those you lead.

1. Empower Your People

The selfless leader embraces this fundamental principle: until you empower your people, they are only spectators. When they are empowered, they can produce, achieve, and succeed. So how do we empower our faculties? How do we help them maximize their potentials? Find opportunities for all of your teachers to take on leadership roles. It may be chairing a committee, representing the school at the board level, or developing professional development for the rest of the faculty based upon an interest or expertise that they have.

2. Be a Thermostat, not a Thermometer

Have you ever met a leader who made a difficult situation worse? These leaders are often influenced by the situation rather than influencing the situation. These are what we call the thermometer leaders. Thermometer leaders reflect or react to their surroundings. When stress levels are running high and people are on edge, these leaders tend to lose their cool. They become irritable, demanding, critical, impatient, and maybe even lose their temper. The thermometer leadership does not inspire trust and commitment with people, but erodes it.

The thermostat leader, on the other hand, has a pulse on the morale, stress level, and environmental conditions of their teachers. When teachers are under pressure from a heavy workload, resources are scarce, or looming tests are causing stress, they cool things off by acting as the calming influence to their team. The thermostat leaders create trust and confidence with their teachers. They never overreact and often respond to situations in a controlled, thoughtful way. The thermostat leaders are always monitoring the school environment, and if the temperature gets too hot or cold, they decide what to do to correct the situation. So, they tend to be more proactive to fend off situations that could become uncomfortable or too tense.

3. Hire and Manage for Strengths

The irony of most hiring is that we seek out candidates who will bring value to the position. We look for people with a strong resume and talents that stand out. However, once we have this perfect candidate in place, the focus becomes more about improving performance or fixing weaknesses than it is about improving the strengths on which they were hired.

One leader shared her experience as a first-year teacher. She was looking forward to bringing her talents and strengths to her new job. However, within the first few weeks of school, she was given something called a PAC, which was a personal appraisal cycle that was meant for her to focus on areas of improvement for the school year. She was required to spend her first-year teaching by focusing on two or three areas that she felt needed improvement. This is not a unique situation when you consider that most employees are evaluated with a performance review, which usually focuses on areas of growth or weakness. If she was hired for her strengths, wouldn't it make sense to focus on developing those strengths to be exceptional, rather than just focusing on the improvement areas? Unfortunately, this is how the education focuses on students as well.

As mentioned earlier, when people are in positions where they feel like they use their strengths, they are six times more productive. So don't limit the success of your teachers by focusing on improving weaknesses, but on developing their strengths. In fact, research by Jack Folkman, author of *How to Be Exceptional*, suggests that what made leaders great was the presence of strengths and not the absence of weaknesses. The reality is that it's our strengths that make us successful and even give us our worth. According to Folkman's research, "leaders have weaknesses, but they don't hurt their leadership if their strengths are their focus" (Zenger and Folkman, 2012, 26). So the lesson here is, don't just hire teachers based upon their strengths, but help them develop their strengths to become exponentially more successful.

4. Have a Passion for Compassion

If there is one remark we hear from teachers consistently, it's that they wish their administration remembered what it was like being a teacher or put themselves in their shoes. Remember the crunch times, such as open house, standardized testing, or implementing a new program. Remember the students who weren't as enthusiastic about school as they should be, or the parents who needed a little extra attention. Think of the situations teachers face and try to be more understanding and compassionate. Do what you can to show that they are valued.

5. Walk the Talk

The story is told of a young boy in the 1930s who had become addicted to and obsessed with eating sugar. No matter how much his mother chided him, he continued to satisfy his sweet tooth. Totally frustrated, she decided to take him to see his hero Mahatma Gandhi. So, they took the long and hot journey walking many miles and hours under the scorching sun.

She finally reached Gandhi and asked him to tell her son to stop eating sugar since it wasn't good for his health. Gandhi listened to the woman carefully and then turned and spoke to her son, "Go home and come back in two weeks." The mother was confused and upset but took the boy home.

Two weeks later she came back. This time Gandhi looked directly at the boy and said "Boy, you should stop eating sugar. It is not good for your health." The boy nodded his head and promised he wouldn't. The boy's mother was puzzled. She asked "Why didn't you tell him that two weeks ago when I brought him here to see you?" Gandhi smiled and said "Mother, two weeks ago I was eating a lot of sugar myself."

While this story may or may not have actually happened, it is applicable to educational leadership. Don't expect your teachers to do anything that you aren't willing to do yourself. If you want your teachers to be supportive of students, then reflect that in how you deal with then. If you want teachers to differentiate instruction, then make sure you are meeting the professional development needs of each teacher, not just the collective whole. On the flipside, if you want teachers who are calm, rational, and introspective, make sure you're reflecting these traits as well. Be consistent and willing to do whatever it takes to make your teachers successful.

6. Build Community

One of the most important roles of an administrator is building community within the school. There are many aspects of community building, such as involving parents more, or engaging more with the business community. But for the sake of this section, let's focus on teachers. One of the easiest ways to build community with teachers is to initiate positive conversations with your staff. We know that we never want the first conversation with a parent to be about a negative experience, such as the student getting in trouble in class. Well, the same is true of your teachers. Don't let the first conversation or most conversations be negative. A Harvard study revealed that there should be about a 6:1 ratio of positive comments to negative comments to be most effective as a leader (https://hbr.org/2013/03/the-ideal-praise-to-criticism).

The former CEO of Avis car rental, Carlos Aquilera, would make a habit of visiting car rental places around the country. He would put ten pennies in his pocket and during the course of the day he would give compliments and praise to his staff and move a penny to the other pocket. That way he knew he gave at least ten positive compliments each day. This is great for two reasons. One, he was focused on giving positive feedback or praise, and second, it meant he had to spend time with his employees. He wasn't tucked away in his CEO office.

When teachers know you're on their side, and support them, then you build a community of trust and loyalty with them. Keep these three things in mind for building positive community with your staff: encourage them to be world class; let them know that you want to hear of issues from them personally; and let them know you have their back.

7. Share Praise, Not Blame

Even if you're not a big football fan, you have probably heard of Nick Saban, head coach of the University of Alabama football team. He has won more National Championships than any other coach in history. While he is a great coach, he may be an even better leader. When his team wins, he shares the praise. He makes comments like, "the players did their job" or "assistant coaches had the players prepared." But most impressive is how he responds to setbacks. When they lose he will rarely blame his players, but will say, "I didn't prepare the players well enough," or "I didn't have them focused," or "I was just out-coached." So share victories with teachers and when things do go wrong, take the responsibility and refocus the staff so you don't make the same mistakes again.

8. Recognize Key Stress Times

Don't overload teachers with professional development during report card season. Don't expect committee work or other duties during conference time. Avoid new initiatives and stresses during the end of the term, report-writing periods, or while teachers are grading exams. If there's any way you can lend a hand during these times, whether it's taking on some of the work yourself, or covering a teacher's lunch supervision shift, help shoulder the load for your team.

9. Keep Requesting Feedback

Selfless leaders welcome feedback, both formally and informally. This may be difficult for some people because we don't like being judged. How you react to the feedback will dictate how your teachers respond in the future as well. So make sure they understand that it is meaningful and that you do take it into account. This doesn't mean that you have to respond to everything that is written, but if you see trends, then it is important to at least reflect on it and here again is an opportunity for teachers to feel like they have a voice.

 Pause to Reflect: What two strategies from that list resonate with you the most? Why?

Hopefully the strategies for becoming a selfless leader have created a shift in your perception of how an educational leader should actually lead. It is about being other-focused. Does your staff have what they need to be successful? And are you utilizing the amazing talents and strengths of your teachers?

Chapter 4: Key Points to Remember

In this chapter, we've discussed what it means to be a selfless leader. You may already exhibit some traits of a servant leader, and you can work on building other traits. Here is a recap to help you improve in this area and put teachers first.

- ◆ **Find out what motivates your staff.** This may mean doing an interest inventory, conducting interviews, or taking the time to just sit down and get to know your staff and what motivates them like the story of Captain Abrashoff.

- **Focus on developing servant leadership traits**. These traits make your teacher the focus. Listen, empathize, build relationships, and build community.
- **Bring your Assets, not your Agenda**. Take the focus off of advancing, more money, or recognition for what we have accomplished, and take an inventory of what you bring to the table to improve your staff. Remember the story of the homeless man.
- **Be a thermostat, not a thermometer.** Be a person of influence. You control the climate of culture of the school, so don't let it control you. Have a pulse on the morale, stress level, and environmental conditions of their teachers, so you can calm high stress situations, or inspire when spirits are waning.
- **Hire and manage for strengths.** You hire people because of the strengths and talents that you feel they bring to your team. So, don't forget this when they get on the team. Seek to develop their strengths to become even better more so than just focusing on the weaknesses.
- **Walk the Talk.** Teachers respect an administration who are willing to jump in and get their hands dirty. Don't expect your teachers to do anything that you aren't willing to do yourself. For example, if you want your teachers to be supportive and understanding with students, then reflect that in how you deal with then. Show them you are in it with them.

5

Inspiring Teachers to Remember Their Purpose

When we think of inspirational leaders, names like Martin Luther King Jr., Mother Theresa, and Gandhi immediately come to mind. We are inspired by their ability and willingness to be selfless, creative, innovative, or authentic. They were ordinary people who decided that the world needed their help and that they had a purpose to fulfill. The beauty of their ordinary beginnings is that it shows anyone can indeed become an inspiring leader.

I am fortunate to have many female relatives in my life who have inspired me and inspired countless other people. One of them was my cousin Jamie Kent Williams. Most of you have never heard of Jamie Williams. However, in her small corner of the world, she was inspiring to many. Jamie was the president of a financial consulting company. Before starting her own company, she was a very successful executive for Wachovia and Wells Fargo banks. What made Jamie successful, however, was not her rise in the financial industry, but rather how she inspired all the people she met. She was dedicated to helping those in need, especially struggling single moms. Jamie created an annual Women's Conference where she inspired women, helped them with financial planning, and encouraged them to improve their own lives by offering them strategies on budgeting, getting more education, and other life skills.

Sadly, Jamie passed away this past summer. But, even in death, she still inspired others by the legacy that she left behind. Hundreds attended her funeral. What was remarkable was the number of people who started their conversations with, "what an inspiration Jamie was" and "how she had helped them out in their time of need." One of her longtime employees and mentees, Susan Reznor Moone, shared what made her so inspirational. She said, "Jamie instilled in me to love people through the process, whether it was a personal or professional matter. She also had high expectations of herself and others. If she thought there was a better way, she would never settle for good enough. She wasn't just my boss, but she was my mentor. My own leadership abilities were greatly influenced by her leadership." Whether it was giving to missions, going on missions, helping struggling families, helping women get back on their feet or learn to stand on their own feet, Jamie was as selfless as any person could be.

Jamie is wonderful examples of an inspirational leader. The word inspire actually comes from the Latin word "inspirare" which means "inspirit" or "divine guidance." There is a spiritual quality to inspiration. It is an inward feeling or driving force that guides you toward something bigger, your purpose, which aligns with your core values. This is different from motivation, for example, which is more of an external force compelling you to action. We need both to maximize our potential, but it's important to understand that they are two different concepts with different driving forces. As mentioned in Chapter 2 on motivation, we can be driven by motives such as pay, position, autonomy, or a myriad of other factors. But inspiration is more about purpose and passion. The key to inspiring others is to be inspired yourself. If you believe you are fulfilling your purpose, then you are more likely to inspire others to fulfill their purpose.

Here's an example of the differences between the terms. Imagine seeing a commercial asking for donations to St. Jude Children's Research Hospital, which treats youth cancer patients.

You might be motivated to give because you want the hospital reach their goal of raising money or because the gift is tax-deductible. But from an inspirational perspective, you give because you feel a desire to help these children in need. You are inspired by the strength of the children in the commercial and you feel empathy, thinking what if that were my child? So, while inspiration is different from motivation, it may be even more important for getting the most from your teachers.

In addition to helping us achieve new goals, inspiration is also good for our general well-being. It can increase feelings of gratitude and appreciation, improve our mood, and provide us with a heightened sense of purpose.

Strengths + Passion = Purpose

They say there are two important days in your life: the day you were born and the day you realize why you born. We were all born with purpose. Our purpose is typically found when we identify and develop our talents and our passions. We have discussed the importance of helping teachers find their strengths so that they will be more successful in their personal and professional life. But there is not much more inspiring than living out your purpose. When you help teachers identify their strengths and passions and utilize them in the classroom and school community, then they will be inspired and inspiring to everyone else.

Strengths

One of the best ways to inspire others is to value them. Our strengths, or the things we do well, are what give us value. Earlier in the book, I discussed focusing on strengths instead of weaknesses, but let's revisit the topic in relation to helping teachers feel inspired. Here are some strategies to develop your teachers' strengths, value, and consequently inspiration.

- ◆ There are several types of tests, such as StrengthsFinders, which will help them identify their strengths.

- ◆ Have one-on-one discussions, like Captain Mike did, to find out what they do well and where their talents and interests lie.
- ◆ When you observe teachers, see what they do well in the classroom. This requires more than the occasional evaluation.

All of this is important because the way teachers teach is shaped by their strengths. "When teachers leverage their strengths in the classroom," says Carol Vernon, certified executive coach, "they are more naturally engaged with their students and students know it!" "One way to identify them to yourself," says Vernon in an interview with We Are Teachers, "is to identify the activities that you do regularly that make you most energized and engaged" (Cleaver, 2013) Strengths are the traits that you find yourself coming back to again and again, regardless of what you may have originally planned. In contrast, the types of activities that you find most draining, or the ones you never do, may rely too much on skills that you have not fully developed. For example, one teacher may thrive at teaching in an active and noisy classroom, while another may prefer to instruct via quieter, more focused classroom discussions. So make sure to give your teachers the freedom to teach to their strengths. This is the great way for the teachers to not only be inspired but to be inspiring!

 Pause to Reflect: Are you remembering to focus on your teachers' strengths and not just their weaknesses?

Passion

There is a joke that says elementary and middle school teachers love their students, high school teachers love the subject, and college professors love themselves. While this is a humorous observation, it does reflect the fact that we need passion with teaching. **Without passion, teaching misses the point.**

This section will help you better understand how to help your teachers ignite their passion in the classroom and in the school. Because let's be honest, do you really want a passionless teacher in your school? This isn't to say that teachers will stand on the desk and get ovations with every lesson. But do you want bored and indifferent teachers in the classroom? These are the clock-watchers, the ones who rush in late, or the ones running to the parking lot at the end of the school day. They love Fridays and, in Garfield fashion, hate Mondays!

So, how do you help teachers use their passions? You can help them find ways to incorporate their passions into their lessons or into other aspects of the school. For example:

- ◆ Enrichment: reading, musical instruments
- ◆ Sports: jogging/walking, fitness/yoga, team sports
- ◆ Social activities: card games, dance movements, drama
- ◆ Creative: drawing, pottery, painting
- ◆ Outdoors: nature walk, adventure or rope elements, hiking.

It's hard to light the fire of learning in a student if the teacher is a wet blanket. So first you have to ignite or reignite their passions for learning and teaching!

 Pause to Reflect: What are your teachers' passions and how can you help ignite them?

Purpose

Whether your teachers are new or veterans of 20 years, you want them to feel like they are fulfilling their purpose in their roles. Our purpose is really our personal mission statement. Much like how a school mission statement should be revisited or recalled to help keep the school moving forward, so too must we develop and reflect on our own personal mission statements, so that we continue to fulfill our purpose of impacting lives. Most teachers will agree that they got into education to make a difference and to impact the lives of their students. This is the foundation for the mission statement or purpose of most teachers. But it can be tough as the school moves along to stay motivated and engaged. So don't take it for granted that your teachers will always be passionate. Help them revisit and revise their mission and purpose from time to time, so they can fulfill that purpose and make a difference in the lives of their students.

Additional Ways to Keep Teachers Inspired

Beyond helping your teachers find and fulfill their purpose, there are other ways to keep teachers inspired. As mentioned earlier, teaching is a service profession. This means that they do see a bigger purpose than just doing a job. It means teachers will endure more, such as lower pay, less resources, because they know the reason for teaching is part of a bigger picture. Keep them inspired, so they will inspire their students. Here are some strategies that will help you create a culture of inspiration for your teachers.

1. Tell Stories

When you are dealing with people, it's important to remember that people connect with stories. You can have tons of data, programs, and even a great school improvement plan, but people remember stories. According to Forbes, Virgin Group founder Richard Branson likes to gather his team around a fire to swap stories. "Storytelling is the best way we have of coming up with new ideas," Branson once said (Gallo, 2016). Branson believes that the ability to sell ideas in the form of story is critical to career and business success. The same is true of building community and building success in education. Find something that has touched your heart recently, whether it's something you read about or something that happened to you.

2. Help Teachers Avoid Burnout

As we've mentioned, teachers are human first, and so there is a need for a new kind of leader who practices inspired, whole person, or purposeful leadership, responsible for mobilizing, focusing, inspiring, and regularly recharging the energy of those they lead. Teacher burnout can occur at many levels, weekly, yearly, seasonally, etc. Many teachers have trouble with the basics: finding time (and coverage) to use the bathroom, to eat lunch, or even to make copies. Teachers have their schedules created without any thought to how they might be affected. Seek teacher feedback when creating schedules, considering that teachers need to take care of themselves, especially during standardized testing and special events. Frustrations with simple and needed tasks can lead to burnout and health problems. One idea is to get the PTA or PTO to have parent volunteers come make copies for teachers. Another great idea to do as the year progresses is to use a PD day to let teachers have family time or play time. Sometimes these "mental health" days helps us reignite our passion!

3. Nurture Greatness
Invite your teachers for one-on-one conversations with you during the first term. Offer them quality coffee or tea. Ask questions and listen to the answers. This will enable you to learn about your teachers' passions, interests, and concerns. You will be able to harness their passions and interests for innovative and creative projects with real buy-in throughout the year or years ahead. This will add significantly to staff morale and your school community. Have small group coffee once a month, with groups such as the teachers from one team or grade level. Make this less formal and listen their concerns, ideas, or just talk about family. One of the best ways for leaders to nurture greatness is simply to focus on your teachers in an uplifting manner.

4. Have High Expectations
The difference between teachers with great classroom management and those with less-than-great management is usually not the number of rules they have, but the expectations they set for their students. The same is true of adults. We often live up to someone's lowest expectations. In the opening story, an employee shared that Jamie had high expectations of herself and her staff.

The same should be true with your faculty. A coach for the University of Florida once said that his players did two things on the field: what he taught them to do and what he allowed them to do. If you allow some teachers to come in late without addressing the issue with them, then this is what you allow them to do and can be seen as permissible. By the same token, when great teachers do great things, recognize them and their work. This will reinforce the high expectations. Also, have high expectations for yourself. You should be the example of doing things the right way at all times. It is very inspiring when your teachers see that you have high expectations for yourself.

5. Be a Mentor

One of the greatest ways to inspire is to serve as a mentor. As Susan mentioned in the opening story, Jamie wasn't just her boss, but she was her mentor. If others look up to and are inspired by you, then make time to mentor those who wish to emulate your success. When considering someone to mentor, you have to make sure that your background and experience aligns with what they hope to achieve. More importantly, you have to ready yourself to be completely open and honest. When people look at you as a mentor, they believe in you completely. If you aren't totally authentic in your advice to them, then you aren't truly helping them.

Some of you may be thinking that you haven't achieved enough yet to be a mentor or to be an inspirational leader because you haven't fully achieved your dream. That is simply not so. No matter how far along you are on the path to greatness, you are further along than someone else. These people, such as your teachers, can certainly use your help and advice.

Small Celebrations Are BIG Wins

While we will discuss incentives and rewards later, this section shows the importance of celebrating small victories to keep your teachers inspired! Often we wait until the end of the year, such as teacher appreciation week, a banquet, or some other "big event" to celebrate successes. Well, over time, the small wins will be forgotten and seem unimportant. Recognizing these small wins is as much about being timely as anything else. In the moment, they help keep us inspired and moving forward.

Rachael Robertson was kind enough to share how she celebrates the little wins in her unusual leadership role. Rachael is a motivational speaker and author of the bestselling book, *Leading on the Edge—Extraordinary stories from the most extreme workplace on the planet.* Unlike most leaders, her office doesn't have the luxury of peers with which to share ideas, an expensive desk, or even high-speed broadband! Her "office" is in the most extreme, hostile environment on Earth: Antarctica. Rachael is an expedition leader and one of the first women to ever lead a yearlong scientific expedition to Antarctica.

She described her experiences being near the South pole. She shared:

> In Antarctica we can't go outside between May and August. For 4 months of the year it's dark, all the wildlife has moved on, we're stuck indoors—so there is absolutely nothing exciting going on. Keeping my team inspired and motivated was critical for morale and mental health. But it taught me that every job can have an Antarctic winter. Every job, even teaching, has a period of time where work is just work. It might be crazy busy, but it's still just work. If you want to keep a team inspired through these periods you need to find a reason to celebrate—recognize milestones and important moments. If you don't have one readily apparent then create one. Find a reason.
>
> In Antarctica we celebrated big events but also the smaller successes such as a month without a power blackout, significant scientific data collection or uninterrupted Internet access with a fully functioning server. Usually it was just a notice written on the whiteboard in the dining hall, for example "great work diesel mechanics, 100 days without a power blackout," or I might mention it at a staff meeting, or maybe mention it privately—it

depends on the person—but it was important to find the time to stop and celebrate. To really acknowledge these moments. **Because these moments create momentum.** They give a sense of progress, moving forward and getting closer to our outcomes.

(Robertson, 2017, direct interview)

So the next time you get into the grind of the school year, look for reasons to celebrate your staff. Because at least you're not sitting in total darkness at the South Pole!

In her book, *The Progress Principle*, Teresa Amabile echoes this sentiment of progress through the celebration of small wins. As she explained,

When we think about progress, we often imagine how good it feels to achieve a long-term goal or experience a major breakthrough. These big wins are great—but they are relatively rare. The good news is that even small wins can boost inner work life tremendously. Many of the progress events our research participants reported represented only minor steps forward. Yet they often evoked outsize positive reactions.

(Amabile, 2011, 119)

These small wins make work more meaningful and inspire us to continue forward. So if a teacher reaches a student who has had issues, celebrate! Affirmation is critical to overall success and even the small wins are wins! Celebrate the small successes because they transform moments into the momentum for great things.

 Pause to Reflect: What are some new ways to inspire teachers that you haven't tried yet? Make it a goal to try one or two soon!

Chapter 5: Key Points to Remember

Inspiration is about making a difference and getting the best out of the people you lead. Make it a daily goal to inspire those you lead. Remember your teachers all have different needs, and different levels of stress on them, but you have the ability to inspire each of them. Also remember that inspiration is not about trying to motivate your teachers, but leading them toward something bigger. Here is a recap of some of the key strategies to help you inspire your teachers so they can inspire others.

- ◆ **Help your teachers identify the Purpose**. Remember: Strengths + Passions = Purpose.
- ◆ **Share and create stories**. We relate to and are inspired by stories.
- ◆ **Celebrate small successes**! Little moments build momentum to bigger things.
- ◆ **Nurture greatness**. Help teachers harness their passion and use it to be creative and innovative in the classroom. Help them become the best they can be.
- ◆ **High Expectations**. Teachers will rise to your level of expectation, especially when they feel like you value and respect them.
- ◆ **Be a mentor**. You have a reached a level of success that your faculty may desire to achieve, so help them along the way. We all need mentors, regardless of the position we hold. Even CEOs often have colleagues they see as mentors, and almost always are willing to give back by mentoring others.

6

Developing Your Emotional Intelligence

When it comes to putting teachers first, this may be the most impactful chapter. This is mainly because Emotional Intelligence is not something that has been viewed as sine qua non (essential or significant) when it comes to leadership. We don't like to think of ourselves as highly emotional people, especially in leadership roles. If I had titled this chapter "Feelings," some of you may have skipped it altogether. But the truth of the matter is that we are emotional beings, and our emotions control more of our actions on a daily basis than even our intellect.

While it would be impossible to count the exact number of emotions we feel per day, research by Debra Trampe, et. al. revealed that everyday human life is profoundly emotional with people experiencing at least one emotion 90% of the time (2015). This means we are almost continually experiencing some type of emotion or emotions. Being a teacher, and teaching in particular, is described as an emotional practice and emotions are characterized as being "an integral part of teachers' lives" (Hargreaves, 1998). So the emotions are there and we need to address them.

Emotions are not a bad thing, as neurologist Antonio Damasio points out in his book, *Descartes Error:* "When emotion is entirely left out of the reasoning picture, as happens in certain neurological conditions, reason turns out to be even more flawed than when emotion plays bad tricks on our decisions" (2005). So emotions are important, and how we control them affects our ability to relate and even lead others.

In fact, high emotional intelligence is often what separates the great leaders from the rest of the leadership pack. That's because most leaders are promoted based on past competencies and not on pure leadership skills. This means they possessed important technical skills and intelligence and performed well in previous roles. However, excelling within the context of relationships, as a leader, requires more than those skills and experiences. So, what is it that makes some leaders stand out—what is the missing link between good and great leaders? Travis Bradberry, author of *Emotional Intelligence 2.0*, believes that emotional intelligence makes the difference. An effective leader needs a high level of emotional intelligence to build strong relationships and teams.

As a school leader, think of successful leaders that you have had yourself. Do you remember them for their ability to handle the budget, or their ability to handle people? You may remember them as being self-aware, calm even in crisis, and encouraging of your work. They might have great relationships with teachers, completely trust staff, be easy to talk to, and always make careful, informed decisions. These are characteristics of someone who exhibits a high level of emotional intelligence.

When it comes to developing relationships and teamwork, a leader's emotional intelligence is more important than his or her IQ. After all, do you think teachers would perform better for a leader who yells and screams when under stress or a leader who is calm and in control, even in stressful situations? You have to set the tone for the school. Research by Barsade showed that in any given group, the most powerful person in the room has the ability to influence the emotions of everybody else (2002). For the work of principals, this means creating an emotional climate that can be characterized by positive interactions among the people within it. This places a significant challenge for principals to serve as the model for strong emotional intelligence.

Create a culture where teachers want to come to school—and you do, too! It's kind of like the mother who comes into her son's room and says, "son, it's Monday. Time to get up! Time to get up and go to school! Get up!" From under the covers he mumbles, "I don't want to go!"

"What do you mean?" she says. "That's silly! Now get up and get dressed and go to school!"

"No!" he shoots back. "I hate school. The students make fun of me and none of the teachers like me. Give me one good reason why I should go to school." The mother replies, "I'll give you two reasons. First, school is important so you should go, and second, you are the principal!" This story always gets a hearty laugh, but it's an important one because it highlights the importance of relationships.

Educational leaders must work cooperatively with a lot of other people, especially teachers. A leader's capacity for social awareness and empathic behavior is essential to creating a high-performing school.

So What Is Emotional Intelligence?

There are five domains of emotional intelligence (EI)—sometimes labeled as (EQ)—that are important to effective leadership and building strong relationship. They are self-awareness, self-regulation (control), empathy, motivation, and social skills. Below are brief descriptions of each domain, as described in *What is Emotional Intelligence (EQ)?* (Akers & Porter, 2003).

- ◆ **Self-awareness**: The ability to recognize an emotion as it "happens" is the key to your EI. If you can evaluate your emotions, you can manage them. The major elements of self-awareness are emotional awareness and self-confidence. Leaders who are more aware of their emotions are able to manage them better, so they can respond more effectively to situations as they arise. Leaders who react from their emotions without filtering them can severely damage relationships and increase mistrust among their staff. In terms of self-awareness, it's particularly important to know if you have an out of control temper, if you ignore input from others when you ask for it, and if you have a "my way or the highway" attitude in your leadership.

◆ **Self-regulation**: You often have little control over when you experience emotions. You can, however, have some say in how long an emotion will last by using a number of techniques to alleviate negative emotions such as anger, anxiety, or depression. A few of these techniques include recasting a situation in a more positive light, taking a long walk, and meditation or prayer. Self-regulation involves traits such as self-control, trustworthiness, conscientiousness, and adaptability.

◆ **Motivation**: To motivate yourself for any achievement requires clear goals and a positive attitude. Although you may have a predisposition to either a positive or a negative attitude, you can, with effort and deliberate practice, learn to think more positively. If you catch negative thoughts as they occur, you can reframe them in more positive terms, which will help you achieve your goals. Your motivation is a combination of achievement, commitment, and optimism.

◆ **Empathy**: This is the ability to recognize how people feel and is important to success in your personal life and career. The more skillful you are at discerning the feelings behind others' behaviors, the better you can control how you respond to them. An empathetic person excels at service orientation, developing others, and understanding others.

◆ **Social skills**: The development of good interpersonal skills is paramount to success in your life and career. In today's always-connected world, everyone has immediate access to technical knowledge. Thus, "people skills" are even more important now because you must possess a high EI to better understand, empathize, and negotiate with others in a global economy. Among the most useful social skills are the ability to influence, to communicate well, to manage conflict, and to collaborate.

 Pause to Reflect: Which of the five domains is your strongest area? Which is your weakest?

A high degree of emotional intelligence brings many benefits. For example, increased self-awareness helps you respond better to day-to-day situations you face personally and professionally, such as a personnel issue or even dealing with traffic on your daily commute. A heightened level of empathy can reduce the duration of these episodes and can lead to a healthier response from the other parties.

Emotional intelligence also translates to optimal outcomes for leaders. In challenging situations such as negotiations and terminations, or even in positive cases such as celebrations or achievements, a high degree of EI can go a long way in building strong relationships with your teachers.

Enhancing Your Emotional Intelligence

Emotional intelligence is something that can be developed and nurtured. It is a flexible skill and one on which you can work. There's a neuronal pathway between the rational and emotional centers of your brain. When you work on your EI, you actually build new neurons, you grow new pathways, or you advance the pathway that increases the flow of information (Bradberry, 2009).

Numerous studies have shown a positive relationship between emotionally intelligent leadership and employee satisfaction, retention, and performance. So, it is important for this to be a focal point of your leadership development and building better relationships with your faculty. Below are a few strategies, including some from *Psychology Today* (Rosenthal, 2012), that will help you improve your EI and improve your overall effectiveness.

- Reflect on your own emotions and consider how you typically respond to situations. For example, how do you respond to a frustrated teacher? How to you respond when someone questions a decision? Do you react negatively? By first identifying your own emotions and reactions, you become more mindful and start the process of building control.
- Get feedback. We don't realize that others may view us much differently than we view ourselves, and vice versa. It's not about right or wrong; it's simply about understanding how we perceive others and are perceived ourselves, and the consequences those differences create. Create an online survey where your teachers can provide feedback anonymously, or have one-on-one meetings with teachers about how you handled a certain situation. Specific feedback will help you grow.
- Listen to your body. A knot in your stomach while driving to work may be a clue that your job is a source of stress. Listening to this type of sensation and the underlying feelings that they signal will allow you to process with your powers of reason. When something is weighing heavily on you, then you probably want to step back and analyze it as rationally as possible so that you aren't going to react to it with raw emotion.
- Ask yourself: How do I feel today? Start by rating your overall sense of well-being on a scale of 0 and 100 and write the scores down in a daily log book. If your feelings seem extreme one day, take a minute or two to think about any ideas or associations that seem to be connected with the feeling. Some days you will have a bad day, and when you are aware of it, you can gauge how much interaction you should have with others or maybe delay certain decisions until another day.
- Know when enough is enough. There comes a time to stop looking inward; learn when it's time to shift your

focus outward. Studies have shown that encouraging people to dwell upon negative feelings can amplify those feelings. Emotional intelligence involves not only the ability to look within, but also to be present in the world around you. This is important when you have to have a tough discussion with a teacher or deal with a program that isn't working properly. We tend to focus too long on the negative. You have to address it, but then move on. Don't let negative feelings continue to follow you.

◆ Make use of the pregnant pause. "The pause" may be as simple as taking a moment to stop and think before acting or speaking. If everyone made that a practice, imagine how much shorter emails could be, how much time would be saved in meetings, and how many provocative comments on social media would be eliminated. This pause is used in public speaking to recapture attention or let your audience know something important is coming. But in conversation it may give you a moment to think through an issue or topic before simply reacting emotionally.

 Pause to Reflect: Pick one of the strategies above for improving your EI and think of one concrete way you can try it this week.

Overcoming the Roadblocks to Improving EI

Decades of research now point to emotional intelligence as being the critical factor that sets star performers apart from the rest of the pack. The connection is so strong that 90% of top performers have high emotional intelligence (Bradberry, 2009). So success is not so much about being the smartest person in the room, but about being able to read the room. In fact as Bradberry discovered in his research, people with average IQs outperform those with the highest IQs 70% of the time. This anomaly threw a massive wrench into the broadly held assumption that IQ was the sole source of success (2009).

Therefore, it is important to understand the roadblocks that may affect your emotional intelligence and how to overcome them. Dr. Travis Bradberry, author of *Emotional Intelligence 2.0*, shares signs of lacking EI. Here are the roadblocks and how to overcome them. (2009)

1. Manage Your Stress

When you stuff your feelings, they quickly build into the uncomfortable sensations of tension, stress, and anxiety. Unaddressed emotions strain the mind and body. Your emotional intelligence skills help make stress more manageable by enabling you to recognize and address tough situations before things escalate.

2. Use Precise Emotional Vocabulary

All people experience emotions, but only a select few can accurately identify them as they occur. People with high EI control their emotions because they understand them, and they use an extensive vocabulary of feelings to do so. While many people might describe themselves as simply feeling "bad," emotionally intelligent people can accurately identify whether they feel "irritable," "frustrated," or "anxious." The more specific your word choice, the better insight you have into how you are feeling, what caused it, and what you should do about it.

3. Avoid Assumptions

People who lack EI form an opinion quickly and then succumb to confirmation bias, meaning they tend to gather evidence that supports their opinion and ignore any evidence to the contrary. This is especially dangerous for leaders, as their under-thought-out ideas become the entire team's strategy. Emotionally intelligent people let their thoughts marinate, because they know that initial reactions are driven by emotions. They give their thoughts time to develop, consider the possible consequences, and include ideas from others in their decision.

Then they communicate their developed idea in the most effective way possible, taking into account the needs and opinions of their audience.

4. Don't Hold Grudges

It is ideal to have a thick skin when you are in a leadership position. People are not always going to agree with you. This doesn't mean you should take it personally or that you should hold a grudge. The negative emotions that come with holding on to a grudge are actually a stress response. Unfortunately, holding on to that stress will negatively affect your body and can have negative health consequences over time. Holding on to a grudge means you're holding on to stress, and emotionally intelligent people know to avoid this at all costs. So let go of grudges if you have them. When in disagreements, focus on the issues and not on the individuals. Never make it personally.

5. Control Your Anger

Emotional intelligence doesn't mean you have to be nice all the time; it's about managing your emotions to achieve the best possible outcomes. Sometimes this does mean showing people that you're upset, sad, or frustrated. Constantly masking your emotions with happiness and positivity isn't genuine or productive. Emotionally intelligent people employ negative and positive emotions intentionally in the appropriate situations. The key is to handle the anger or frustrations tactfully and professionally. No outbursts! This includes managing your emotional triggers. These are the situations and people that push our buttons and cause us to act impulsively. As you become more self-aware, you will study your triggers and use this knowledge to sidestep situations and people before they get the best of you.

6. Learn to Anticipate

Emotionally intelligent leaders are able to anticipate how their staff is likely to react to tough situations. They don't wait until after the damage is done to respond. Realizing that rumors can quickly spread and cause more damage than the actual event, strong leaders rely upon their emotional and social skills to help staff through these times.

7. Explore the "Why"

Most of us would agree that empathy and compassion are valuable components to healthy relationships. So why do we often neglect to show those qualities when it matters most—like when we fail to show understanding to a teacher when he or she is going through a difficult time? We often forget how specific situations feel, even if we've experienced very similar circumstances. Never forget to put yourself in someone else's shoes before judging him or her. Ask yourself, questions like: why is the person feeling this way? What am I not seeing that I should?

Relational Intelligence

Relational intelligence is a combination of emotional and ethical intelligence. This means that it is more than just emotions, but it includes our own and others' values, interests, and demands, which we reflect critically upon and use to guide our action and behavior with respect to people.

Jeremie Kubicek, author of the book *5 Gears: How to Be Present and Productive When There Is Never Enough Time*, calls relational intelligence the future competitive advantage for leaders. Jeremie says, "Relational intelligence is the ability to connect and be present in the midst of tasks" (Kubicek, 2015, 19). For instance, how many times have you been in a conversation with someone only to be distracted or to notice they are distracted? One example may be talking with someone who checks his phone or is replying to an email. This is not good relational intelligence. To be in the moment is to give someone your full attention.

And it's important to not only be in the moment, but to make sure you have the time to engage someone fully as well. As an administrator, have you ever had a teacher pop into your office to ask a question? According to Kubicek, a person with high relational intelligence may react to an interruption by saying: "I would love to talk about this, but my mind is focused on something else at the moment and I'm not going to be fully with you right now. Can we meet at 2 p.m. when I can be fully focused on you?" (2015). Being intentional, wanting to be present, that's relational intelligence.

Finally, you have to know when to switch modes. For example, when you leave work, do you switch off work mode to family mode? This is part of relational intelligence. Don't bring your work home. How often have you gotten home only to spend another hour on the phone or respond to messages while you family is waiting on you to engage with them?

The Story of the Worry Tree

The carpenter I hired to help me restore an old farmhouse had just finished a rough first day on the job. A flat tire made him lose an hour of work, his electric saw quit, and now his ancient pickup truck refused to start. While I drove him home, he sat in stony silence.

On arriving, he invited me in to meet his family. As we walked toward the front door, he paused briefly at a small tree, touching the tips of the branches with both hands. When opening the door, he underwent an amazing transformation. His tanned face wreathed in smiles and he hugged his two small children and gave his wife a kiss.

Afterward he walked me to the car. We passed the tree and my curiosity got the better of me. I asked him about what I had seen him do earlier.

"Oh, that's my trouble tree," he replied. "I know I can't help having troubles on the job, but one thing for sure, troubles don't belong in the house with my wife and the children. So I just hang them on the tree every night when I come home. Then in the morning I pick them up again."

"Funny thing is," he smiled, "when I come out in the morning to pick 'em up, there ain't nearly as many as I remember hanging up the night before."

This story is reflective of a high level of relational intelligence where the carpenter was able to transition from professional to personal life. This is a very important skill for you to incorporate as a leader and to ensure that your teachers incorporate as well. For example, don't send emails in the evening, so that teachers won't feel the need to check emails or to respond to you.

 Pause to Reflect: Are there ways you can strengthen your relational intelligence with regard to your staff (and beyond)? Explain.

EI in Schools Across the Globe

As you can see, emotional intelligence can lead to better relationships, more engaged teachers, and a positive school culture. In the US, we don't seem to be focusing on EI within our schools. But others countries have focused on its importance. For example, the Ontario Principals' Council's "Leadership Study" (2005) examined the connection between emotional intelligence and principal/vice-principal performance, as rated by staff and their supervisor. It conclusively demonstrated that specific emotional and social competencies are prerequisite characteristics for effective leadership. Their research regarding effective leadership indicates that building leadership capacity in emotional and social competencies is at the foundation of school improvement efforts (Stone, Parker, & Wood, 2005).

In Hong Kong, educator Robin Cheung discussed the importance of Emotional Intelligence for administrators. In the *South China Morning Post*, he said, "School heads have to find ways to motivate and mobilise teachers. . . . *They* have to be able to read moods and emotions, and understand their origins and strengths, especially the negative ones, like the fear of the unknown or unfamiliar. Knowing staff's anxieties arising from change, *they* are in a better position to help them learn new things and relearn or unlearn ineffective ways" (Chueng, 2015). Emotional Intelligence is essential to effective leadership and to putting teachers first to build high-performing schools.

Chapter 6: Key Points to Remember

- ◆ **Increase your self-awareness of your own emotions**. Understanding your emotions and how you react to situations will make you a better leader.
- ◆ **Learn to manage stress**. Administration is a stressful job. Make sure you manage your stress so that you can control your emotions. Exercise, eat healthfully, and practice relaxation techniques.
- ◆ **Increase your emotional vocabulary**. The more words you learn to express emotions and to connect with the emotions of others, the better you will be in relating to others or at least being empathetic to them.
- ◆ **Control anger**. It is okay to have conflict and disagreements. But never make it personal and never let your emotions cause you to overreact.
- ◆ **Be in the moment**. Don't get distracted when in conversation, such as checking text or emails. This shows that you don't value the person you're talking to, even if that is not your intention.
- ◆ **Make time for full attention**. If you are finishing a report or another task, simply let the person know that he or she is important and that you want to meet, but later would allow you to offer your full attention.
- ◆ **Quitting time**. Know when to switch off from work mode and allow teachers to as well. You could work 24 hours a day and still not get everything done. And everything will be at work waiting on you the next morning as well as the teachers. So, make sure off time is valued by you and your teachers.

7

Communicating and Connecting Effectively

The story is told of a passenger in a taxi who tapped the driver on the shoulder to ask him a question. The driver screamed, lost control of the cab, nearly hit a bus, and drove up over the curb, stopping inches from a large storefront window. For a few moments, everything was silent in the cab. Then the driver said, "Please don't do that! You scared the daylights out of me." The passenger, who was also frightened, apologized and said he didn't realize a tap on the shoulder could startle someone so much. The driver replied, "I'm sorry, it's really not your fault. You see, today is my first day driving a cab. But for the past 25 years, I have driven a hearse."

While this is a humorous story, there's a lesson we can learn from it. As a leader, are you driving a taxi or a hearse? Are you in constant communication with your teachers, or would you freak out if one tapped you on the shoulder to speak? If you are not constantly engaging and connecting with your faculty, speaking and listening to them, then you might as well be driving the proverbial hearse.

Communication is really all about relating or connecting to other people. In fact, one definition of communication states that it is a means of connection between people. Unfortunately, communication can sometimes be a one-way street, traveling down from administrators to staff. But that isn't true communication: that's just giving directives and imparting information, such as a newspaper or a weather report. Real communication takes place when both people in a conversation have a chance not only to understand but also to be understood. Communication should never be solely top-down, or in one direction; it should be multi-directional.

Why is communication so important? Effective communication has been identified as one of the top five traits of successful schools (Verdugo & Schneider, 1999). Remember teachers are human first, and communication is probably the most important life skill that we possess, so make sure you're not only making use of this skill, but developing it within your staff. Effective communication will build lasting relationships, improve trust, and increase engagement.

After all, how can you effectively appreciate, motivate, and inspire your teachers if you do not communicate effectively? How they can let you know their needs? Moreover, how can you empower your teachers if they have no voice in the decision-making process? For the purpose of this book, and the teachers-first theme, let us examine how to communicate in a way that makes you more **connected** with your teachers.

The Importance of What Is Said and How It's Said . . . and What Is Not Said

Remember the story of the USS Benfold and how two captains communicated very differently with the same crew? One captain was more of a boss directing everyone, and the other was a connector who listened to his crew. It's amazing that essentially the same group of people took one of the lowest performing ships in the Navy and made it the highest performing, thanks in large part to how the captain communicated with them. So make sure you are constantly aware of what you say and how you say it. It will be the difference in a mediocre school and a great school!

It's important to communicate accurately, consistently, and fairly with your teachers. Teachers appreciate good communication coming from administrators. It produces a healthy work environment. Failing to communicate effectively leads to frustration and confusion among the staff. In addition, as a selfless leader, you are most effective when you are focused on maximizing your staff. This requires effective communication in what you say and how you say it—and in what you don't say!

What Is Said

While there are many settings for communicating, such as one-on-one, small groups, large groups, or even virtually, simplicity is the key. Keeping it simple, clear, and focused optimizes the connection. Good communicators respect people's time and choose simple, straightforward words.

Begin with the "**why**." Whenever you're at work, you're wasting time and effort if you don't know the reason a communication is taking place. Before you initiate any communication, ask yourself, "Why is this important?" Even casual conversation should have a purpose, even if it's just to build camaraderie with your team.

Next you want to focus on the "**what**." What is it all about? Teachers need the details of the issue so they can then work out the implications and requirements for themselves. Have a reason for saying what you are going to say, and don't stray from that. The more you focus on the purpose, the shorter your conversation will be, and the more likely it is that the listener will remember what was said. Most of the time, people don't care about what you're saying unless you're saying something they find valuable on a personal level. That personal level doesn't have to be deep, it just has to exist. Good communicators establish a personal connection by focusing on how their message may impact the other person.

Finally, in most cases, communication includes a call to action. Your teachers need to know how to respond to the information. They may understand what it's about but need to know how they are required to respond. Some may simply ask, "what do I need to do," while others may ask, "What if?" and want to explore more. How they respond depends on many factors, including their strengths. Some may need a challenge to go and do something and learn from the experience. Others may simply need a pointer on how to begin and get it done.

 Pause to Reflect: When you communicate, are you clear about the why, the what, and the what now?

What Is Not Said

What is left out or not said can depend on several factors. Things can be omitted inadvertently or on purpose. For instance, did you see a teacher with a great lesson but missed the opportunity to tell her great job? This isn't done on purpose, but it is still left unsaid. And the truth is that even when something is left unsaid, it still communicates a great deal. With no praise or positive feedback, the teacher may think she isn't valued, when perhaps you were just rushing to a meeting or had something else on your mind. But by not communicating in specific situations, we are communicating something: perhaps that we are shy, perhaps that we are upset, too busy, or that something isn't valued. Ignoring somebody is still communicating with him or her. Since empowering and developing your teachers is hopefully one of your main goals, make sure to take time for them and give praise and positive feedback as often as possible. Remember the 6:1 praise rule we discussed previously.

Another aspect of what is not said involves the assumptions you make when communicating. This may be because you assume your teachers already know the topic of discussion or have the same view on a topic as you. This may cause you to gloss over or leave out information that may be important. For example, you may be discussing the implementation of a new program where you have spent hours studying and discussing it. When you present it to your teachers, you may assume that they know as much as you, so you may leave out key information. The confusing part here is that teachers "don't know what they don't know," so they can't ask for clarification or for more information to make a decision or begin a task.

Sometimes, things are not said because leaders want to hold onto information. Leadership expert and bestselling author Jason Jennings believes in today's culture that knowledge kept in secrecy, or the holding on to knowledge, is the currency of the unproductive. These are the people who only have value because of the secrets they know. He shared that leaders may keep secrets because it gives them a sense of self-importance. But great leaders understand that it's not knowledge, but execution of knowledge, that makes organizations successful (Johnson & Zimmerman, 2018). This doesn't mean you have to share everything you know. If there is information that doesn't benefit teachers or doesn't help them in their duties, you aren't really keeping that information from them.

So, remember that information alone is not power. Rather than trying to hoard your knowledge, share it. Two people will collectively know more than one. Three will know more than two. And when you have a room full of smart people sharing their knowledge, there's very little you can't accomplish together. The flawless execution of knowledge is powerful.

 Pause to Reflect: Do you hold things back that should be communicated more often?

How It's Said

How you communicate may be even more important than what you are communicating. How you communicate is usually how your teachers receive the information. For instance, did you speak in a negative or a positive tone? When giving a directive to your teachers, a statement such as "**teachers must**" is always received more poorly than a statement that says "**we need teachers to.**" Many factors influence how you communicate. Remember your goal is to connect, so keep the "How it's said" positive in word and tone. Remember that teachers already feel like there is a lot on their plate, so be careful how you introduce more. They may be on the defensive already, so you have to win them over. Here are a few of the nonverbal cues that influence how you speak. Be aware of these cues so that you don't cause confusion or send mixed messages.

- *Body Movements* (*kinesics*), for example, hand gestures or nodding or shaking the head
- *Posture*, or how you stand or sit, whether your arms are crossed, etc.
- *Eye Contact*, where the amount of eye contact often determines the level of trust and trustworthiness
- *Para-language*, or aspects of the voice apart from speech, such as pitch, tone, and speed of speaking
- *Closeness or Personal Space* (*Proxemics*), which determines the level of intimacy
- *Facial Expressions*, including smiling, frowning and even blinking
- *Physiological Changes*, for example, sweating or blinking more when nervous.

Another aspect of the "how it's said" can be the actual type of delivery. You can communicate in person, by email, or through several other methods. In today's tech rich culture, there are many different ways to communicate. Remember that your time and your teachers' time is very valuable, so only call meetings when necessary.

When you have to communicate highly **emotional content,** it should be delivered in person. Note that emotional content doesn't have to be something negative. If you've got exciting news, it will be more effective and create more positive energy if you deliver it in person. A group meeting to announce a big news is like an instant celebration. By contrast, an email announcing the same thing seems more like an afterthought. Similarly, if you've got bad news or a criticism, it will be better received, and more likely to be helpful, if it's delivered in person. If you use email, it will seem like you don't care or that you're afraid to address the issue.

On the other hand, any communication primarily consisting of **factual content** should be communicated in writing. People only retain a small percentage of facts when they're communicated verbally. Therefore, having a written record of those facts helps ensure that they don't get lost when it's time to make decisions. Communicating facts verbally to large groups is extremely inefficient. It's much better to use email to get everyone up to speed and then have a discussion of what still needs to be accomplished. Email is a great way to communicate basic information. It is, however, a horrible way to have a strong discussion with a colleague. Remember that once you hit the "send" button, all that you have written in email will never be erased or forgotten. So keep the emails to just the facts! Using emails for facts and informational purposes helps limit the number of faculty meetings that you have to hold, which will make your teachers very grateful!

 Pause to Reflect: Do you use the right format (in person, email, etc.) for the right context? What might you do differently?

Strategies for Building Deeper Connections

Did you know that leaders who can't connect with their people actually work 20% to 30% harder than leaders who can? (http://leadingwithintent.com/). Imagine that by simply improving your ability to connect with staff, your workload becomes more manageable! Now imagine how much more productive your teachers will be when you do make that connection. Communication is not only an important life skill, but is the most important skill for building relationships with your teachers. It is about building trust, respect, and a commitment to developing those you lead. Effective communication makes your teachers feel valued and connected. Here are a few strategies that will help deepen your connection!

1. Start by Evaluating Yourself

As the leader, the whole communication culture begins with you. So, take some time and examine your existing communication skills. For example, take a day or a week and keep track of everyone you came in contact with during the day (that includes texts, emails, newsletters, videochat, everything). Take notes not only on who you communicated with, but also on what the subject matter was, how you believe you communicated (effectively? efficiently? positively?), and on what your takeaway was from each encounter. Finally, do some analysis. Examine the information you've compiled and see if there are any recurring themes. Is there anything you can work on or change? Remember this is one of the most important skills we all possess and deserves to be reflected upon from time to time to make us better communicators.

2. Get Feedback From Teachers

Ask your teachers how you're doing. After all, they are the ones who benefit the most from your ability to communicate. Ask them to answer a survey or email you with their thoughts, or even have an informal discussion with them in person. Keeping an open-door policy is a great way to get feedback—just make sure that teachers actually feel comfortable enough to use it. If you say your door is always open, but your actions scream Unavailable!, Do Not Enter!, I'm Busy!, or if your teachers fear punishment for speaking their minds, you're not actually going to benefit from feedback and you might as well post a sign, Out to Lunch. In addition, if any of the feedback is less than positive, learn to be objective about personal critiques. Don't take them personally, but as an opportunity to become an even more effective leader. If you want to be an effective leader, it's vital that you demonstrate a willingness to act on feedback. You have to reflect on the feedback and see if there are areas in which you can improve or even areas of strength that you can utilize more.

3. Connect for Buy-Ins

When introducing a new policy or initiative, do your best to make teachers feel included, even if it's something that's mandatory. Make the change feel more like a conversation than a directive. We are aware that there simply isn't enough time in the day or week to have deep discussions about everything, but remember teachers want to have a voice in some matters. Use your best judgment, but remember, the more teachers feel ownership, the more they will respond positively. Simply telling them this is the way it is, or that "it's all about the students" is not effective communication and will leave teachers feeling unimportant and disgruntled. Also, don't try to oversell something or embellish it, because they will see through this at some point. Be genuine and upfront and you will be more likely to have their support.

4. Be Trustworthy

Communication is the best way to instill trust in your teachers. Are you generally true to your word? Do your teachers trust that you're doing your best to make the best changes for your school? Are you constantly communicating your ideas and vision to your team? If teachers feel you are doing right by them, it improves morale and productivity. If, for example, your school doesn't have the resources to help teachers do their jobs properly, make sure your staff knows and sees that you are pulling every last string you can find to help get them more resources.

5. Stay Positive

Maintaining a positive attitude is crucial to productive communications. Be constructive rather than being negative or complaining. People shut down when they feel attacked or criticized. Be encouraging and kind, even when expressing concerns or displeasure. Positive communication is contagious and brings out the best in yourself and in those around you. When you practice positive communication, people are more likely to listen to you, the conversation goes better, and the results can be transforming. And never forget to smile. A lot!

6. Give Praise

Some leaders may not be comfortable giving praise, or may think that it's not all that effective. But people like to hear their names associated with something positive. Well-delivered praise increases the likelihood that people will continue the praiseworthy behavior. As we've said earlier, praise should be immediate, so that it is connected to the event, and it should be specific. Don't just say "good job," but explain what actually occurred and why it matters. Pointing out the impact of what they did creates better employee engagement and a greater sense of commitment, and it greatly increases that likelihood that the praise will be remembered.

7. Show You Care

Recognize every employee's birthday in some way. Send cards or gifts for new babies and weddings. Be involved in employees' lives to let them feel loved and valued not only as employees, but as human beings. When people know you truly care, they will inevitably work harder for you. As already discussed, incorporate handwritten notes, make public announcements for praise, and use other ways to show you care. The whole concept of Putting Teachers First is that teachers are the lifeblood of the school. We want to make taking care of them our highest priority and ensure they are as happy as possible at all times.

8. Use Humor

Humor is an effective communication tool. In fact, Dwight Eisenhower once said, "A sense of humor is part of the art of leadership, of getting along with people, of getting things done" (Smith, 2013). Sometimes we get so focused on goals, initiatives, testing, and all the other minutia of education that we forget to enjoy the wonderful relationships of our colleagues.

The first rule of humor, however, is "Do No Harm." Laughter at someone else's expense can harm relationships. Sarcasm, ridicule, and put-downs are not humor; they're just hurtful. Make sure the humor is never at the expense of anyone—except yourself. Learning to laugh at yourself is a good thing. Taking yourself too seriously can create an unfriendly environment where people "walk on eggshells" and never develop a deeper connection. If you can learn to laugh at yourself, you will never be short of humorous material. Self-deprecating humor lowers the walls between yourself and others and can be disarming.

Make sure that your humor is related to the conversation or the occasion. If you do have a rehearsed story, wait until the conversation leads to a good insertion point. You can also direct the conversation in a way that allows you to insert your funny story. Humorous stories are great ice breakers, stress relievers, and learning tools.

9. Be the Lead Communicator About Your School

Be the chief storyteller for your school. Celebrate your teachers to the community. Social media allows parents, community leaders, and the whole community to hear and see your school's story quickly and easily. Are you promoting your teachers and all the great things they do at school? If you don't communicate about your school, someone else will. So make sure you're sharing all the great things in your school. When you visit classrooms, take pictures and share the stories that you see on a daily basis. Show the passion teachers have, such as outdoor learning or team building. Did a teacher write a book, or finish their PhD, or complete some other milestone? Let the community know!

Listen to Connect

Have you ever had a conversation with someone where you said very little but at the end, she told you how much she enjoyed the conversation? This is because you took the time to listen. One of the most effective communication skills is listening. Remember that communication is about connecting, and you can't connect if you don't listen to your teachers. The difficulty with being a good listener is that it makes us focus on others, and by nature we tend to be focused on ourselves. But the beauty of listening is that your teachers, the experts, have feedback, ideas, and suggestions that they would like to share with you. One of the best ways to show them they are important is to listen. Listening to understand and relate is a mindset—not just a skill set.

In today's world of social media, we tend to have more distractions, and those distractions interfere with our ability to focus and listen. But the selfless leader wants to not only listen to their staff but really connect with them. To serve is dependent upon our ability to listen and perceive the needs of others. We serve by creating a space where individual voices can be heard and validated. Here are a few listening strategies to try the next time you're conversing with teachers.

1. Listen to Relate, Not Respond

Usually when we communicate with others, we are more interested in our own thoughts, feelings, and viewpoints. Even when we are actively engaged in a conversation, it is more about waiting to give our response than about relating to what they are saying. Stephen Covey, author of The *7 Habits of Highly Successful People*, once said, "Most people do not listen with the intent to understand; they listen with the intent to reply" (2004, 240). To really connect, we have to focus more on listening to relate. That means understanding what the speaker is trying to convey, the emotions being expressed, and what the person is hoping to achieve through the conversation. In essence, it is about them! Here are a few ways to move from listening to respond to listening to relate and understand.

- ◆ *Get rid of outside distractions.* How many times have you been interrupted in a conversation by a phone dinging, ringing, or binging? It is impossible to focus, much less truly relate, if your attention is distracted. Put everything down and shut off all technology. Relax, get comfortable, and focus.
- ◆ *Don't interrupt.* Have you ever had someone try to talk over you? It can be quite frustrating. Until the person has finished speaking, don't talk—even if they say something that causes a reaction in you and you're tempted to interrupt. You can always go back to a point and respond later.
- ◆ *Keep an open mind.* Don't judge what they say, just listen. You will have time to process the information and you will get an opportunity to respond. But remember the key is to relate, so keep an open mind to their ideas. They may present valid points that you may not hear if you are busy thinking of your response.

♦ *Use attentive cues.* Look the speaker in the eyes. Lean in to show attentiveness. Also, pay attention to the speaker's nonverbal cues. Does their body language and other cues match their words? This indicates trust, honesty, and other details.

2. Build Rapport

Listening enables you to establish rapport with someone. It proves to them that you are interested in them. Rapport is built by having things in common; this makes the communication process easier and usually more effective. People feel valued when they feel like they have been heard and when they feel a genuine connection with you. Meet individually as time allows, or even meet with small groups if that is more feasible. Just making the effort will go a long way with your teachers.

3. Hold Aspirational Conversations

This is an area that can show how much you value your teachers. As we know, most teacher evaluations use the sandwich approach. This is where we say something good, then focus on areas of growth, and they say something nice as they walk out the door, sometimes deflated just because of the process. While an occasional evaluation may be needed, we also need to have what are known as "aspirational conversations" with teachers. These are analogous to formative assessments (ongoing, interim) in place of summative assessment (the test, the autopsy to determine if one passed or failed). There are five key questions to ask staff on a regular basis, during such formative, aspirational conversations.

♦ Have we kept our promises to you?
♦ What do you think we do really well, such as at school do we do reading, extracurricular, etc.?
♦ What do you see such as in other schools that would make us do better?
♦ What would make you want to leave us?
♦ Where do you see yourself in three to five years? People often leave because there is no room to grow. Ask

them about their vision. Do they desire to work toward an administrative role? Tell them you will help them get there. What teacher isn't going to give you their all when they know you have their best interests at heart?

 Pause to Reflect: Do you have conversations with teachers apart from evaluations? If not, how might you schedule some aspirational chats on a regular basis?

The Truth About Confrontations

Confrontation is often seen as a four-letter word. In reality, when people are involved, even in the best school cultures, conflicts will arise. Conflict is kind of like stress. It's not that we will never encounter it, but it is how we deal with it that matters. While confronting someone is not really pleasant, it's something you must do as a leader, and how you do it makes all the difference. One trait of effective leaders is that they are skilled in handling confrontations.

According to Dianna Booher, a communication expert and author of *Speak with Confidence*, leaders must believe that confrontation can be a positive situation. After all, confrontation handled well has many benefits:

 ◆ Innovative solutions to problems
 ◆ Improvements to the status quo
 ◆ Stronger confidence in implementing ideas
 ◆ Stronger relationships
 ◆ Greater harmony
 ◆ Improved communication
 ◆ Better teamwork
 ◆ Greater understanding
 ◆ Increased engagement on the job
 ◆ Strong passion and commitment to see success of the ideas developed (Direct interview with Dianna Booher. Dec. 2017).

So don't shy away from conflict when it arises, but rather use the opportunity to build stronger relationships with your teachers. The reason confrontation is hard is that it is outside our comfort zone. We let things build until emotions are high, and then we tend to overreact. Here are some great strategies to help you deal with conflict better and actually make it a beneficial part of the communication process.

1. Focus on Being Proactive, Not Reactive

Imagine that you have a teacher who is consistently late. Okay, some of you don't have to imagine because you have a teacher who is excessively late. Do you react by sending out a mass email stating that all teachers must arrive on time? When you address it in this manner, the odds of the person correcting their behavior is slim. More than likely, you are going to hurt the morale of the whole staff, because good teachers will remember that one time in a snowstorm that they were two minutes late. And they will dwell on this negativity the rest of the day, or maybe even week. And the teacher who is late? Well, he won't give it another thought, because you didn't address him specifically, so he assumes you are talking about someone else. Never be reactive to this type of situation. Reactive is when you let your emotions control the situation. Being proactive means that you let your sound judgment take control of the situation.

When posed with this scenario, Dianna Booher shared the following:

> Leaders will do well to learn to give direct, straight-forward feedback to individuals. In general, praise in public; coach on negative situations in private. Take the example of teachers who frequently arrive late. If 99 percent of your staff arrive on time throughout the year, you might want to send a mass email to thank them for their continually commitment to punctuality, say how much your appreciate this because it sets a good example for students, and ensures that they are prepared for the day. Then for the few who are routinely tardy, have coaching conversations with them individually. Ask their reasons

for their routine tardiness. Is it that they have a first-period planning and don't feel like they need to arrive at regular time? Do they drop off an elderly parent for therapy at a local nursing home? Do they just not get up in time to get to work? Again, state the expectation, discover if they have an excuse or a real reason for their tardiness. If you're dealing with a reason, brainstorm for creative solutions. Restate the expectation and get their agreement to meet that expectation. Let them know what next steps might be if they fail to meet the agreed-upon standard. Most likely, if they have a reason (versus an excuse), you will have agreed upon a creative solution and the "next steps" part of the conversation may be unnecessary.

(Booher, 2017, direct interview)

As Dianna suggests, there may be times when tough conversations have to occur, and next steps may be needed to correct the issue. Just make sure it is not something that affects the entire staff. Be proactive in praising good behavior, and be proactive in getting ahead of major issues by confronting the person individually.

2. Focus on Relating, Not on Being Right

When we let issues stew, we let our emotions take control. It becomes no longer about the issue, but about being right. Even in the midst of communicating, each person is not really listening to each other, but waiting for a turn to speak, or interrupting to make a point. Try to remember that it's not about being right, it's about relating.

In fact, when you as the administrator begin these tough conversations, your goal should not be to win the argument, but to relate and come to some kind of solution. There is a reason they're called RELATIONships and not RIGHT-ships. You have to be willing to relate to the person, even if that person is wrong. One important point for leaders to remember is that if you have to use your position of power to win an argument, then you really haven't won. You could be seen as a bully and not as someone who is willing to compromise and resolve issues. Some may think that the topic of bullying is not important, but in a recent survey of medium-sized school districts, 25% of employees reported that they had been bullied (Long, 2012).

Yes, 25% of teachers felt their administrators had bullied them. A key area to remove this perception is in handling conflicts better and focusing on relating rather than being right.

3. Focus on the Issue, Not on the Individual

When conflict arises, it could be more about the personalities of the individuals than about the actual issues. You have to distinguish between the two. For instance, weak leaders don't necessarily like strong teachers because they see them as a threat. So conflict may arise when these teachers inevitably speak their mind on a topic. But when dealing with the issue, rather than the individual, what we are saying is that you should focus on the behavior at the root of the conflict and not on the personality of the individuals. If Jim is always late for school, is Jim lazy? Or does Jim lack time management skills? One is a focus on the individual; one is a focus on his behavior.

When focusing on the issue, there is no real solution if we take the perspective that Jim is lazy. In fact, challenging the person and not the behavior will make them defensive and make the situation more difficult. But if we look at the behavior, then we can find solutions to correct behavior. Challenging the behavior and not the person allows for a shared review of the behavior that caused the issues or concern, and there is less likelihood of defensiveness in the person whose behavior is challenged.

4. Focus on the Future, Not on the Conflict

One of two things results from conflict. Either there is some sort of compromise and a solution to the issue, or maybe there is no resolution and there has to be the "next steps" conversation. Hopefully, you reach a compromise more often than not. However, if there needs to be a next step, then that has to be addressed without a personality conflict. Make sure your teachers know that it is not personal and that correcting a problem or issue is all that matters to you.

Think of communication as walking or running. There's a difference between being able to do it and being able to do it well. The same is true of communication. We can all do it, but how many of us do it really well? It is a skill that needs to be developed. The better we communicate and connect with our faculty, the more successful everyone will be.

Chapter 7: Key Points to Remember

- **Focus on what's said, how it's said, and what is not said.** Make sure your communication is clear and concise, and that you aren't sending mixed signals between words and body language to confuse the listener.
- **Don't be afraid of confrontation.** Confrontation is never fun, but being afraid of it may be more detrimental to the group, individuals, etc. Just remember to focus on issues and not the individual. Confrontation and conflict is more about compromise than it is being right.
- **Nonverbal cues matter more than verbal statements.** So be aware of facial expressions, voice inflections, body orientation, etc.
- **Be the chief storyteller**. People love stories and connect with stories. To make sure you tell the story you want told for your school. Whether it is through social media, business interactions, or even the story you tell of your teachers. Make sure the community connects with you and your school positively.
- **Listen for deeper connection**. Listening is not an active process. Make sure you give attention to conversation with a goal of understanding, not simply to reply. Focus on the speaker and what they are saying and how they are saying it.
- **Praise your teachers**. . . . Often!

8

Building a Cohesive Team

You may have heard how geese make such great teammates. They are not focused on the individual but on the team. Even in flight, it is about working together as a team. For example, when each bird flaps its wings, it creates an uplift for the bird immediately following. By flying in a "V" formation, the whole flock adds at least 71% greater flying range than if each bird flew on its own. When a goose falls out of formation, it suddenly feels the drag and resistance of trying to go it alone—and quickly gets back into formation to take advantage of the lifting power of the bird in front.

When the head goose gets tired, it rotates back in the wing and another goose flies point. It is sensible to take turns doing demanding jobs, whether with people or with geese flying south. Geese honk from behind to encourage those up front to keep up their speed.

Finally, when a goose gets sick or is wounded by gunshot, and falls out of formation, two other geese fall out with that goose and follow it down to lend help and protection. They stay with the fallen goose until it is able to fly or until it dies, and only then do they launch out on their own, or with another formation to catch up with their group.

What can we learn from the geese as it pertains to teamwork? The lead goose is leading them in the right direction and will let others lead when necessary

- ◆ They migrate at a specific time to a specific place, so they have a clear vision and goals.
- ◆ Working as a team allows them to accomplish more and more efficiently than attempting it alone.
- ◆ They encourage the leader and others when they are in formation.
- ◆ No goose is left behind. Team members are always there to support each other.
- ◆ Everyone has an important role; no team member is not valued.

The most valuable resource to the geese is the other geese. **The most valuable resource you have as an administrator is your teachers**. They are a wealth of knowledge and experience. They are also the most valuable resource to other teachers. And we become exponentially more valuable when we work as a cohesive team. But when we think of teams, it is important to make a distinction between a group and a team. Remember that the geese weren't just all flying together in a group; there was order and purpose to their flight.

Do you have a group of teachers who work together at times but never as a cohesive team? Building a team is not about a group of people working in the same building or serving together on committees, but is about creating a dynamic organism that has the same goals and is there to support each other in the achievement of those goals. There is a huge difference between a group and a team (see Table 8.1). Here are a few key differences between a group mentality and team mentality in your school (NDT Resource).

As you can see, there are some important distinctions between groups and a team. The team is much more relationship-focused. Teams understand that they have influence beyond

TABLE 8.1 Group vs. Team Traits

Groups	Teams
◆ Members work independently and they often are not working toward the same goal.	◆ Members work interdependently and work toward both personal and team goals, and they understand these goals are accomplished best by mutual support.
◆ Members focus mostly on themselves because they are not involved in the planning of their group's objectives and goals.	◆ Members feel a sense of ownership toward their role in the group because they committed themselves to goals they helped create.
◆ Members are given their tasks or told what their duty/job is, and suggestions are rarely welcomed.	◆ Members collaborate together and use their talent and experience to contribute to the success of the team's objectives.
◆ Members are very cautious about what they say and are afraid to ask questions. They may not fully understand what is taking place in their group.	◆ Members base their success on trust and encourage all members to express their opinions, varying views, and questions.
◆ Members do not trust each other's motives because they do not fully understand the role each member plays in their group.	◆ Members make a conscious effort to be honest, respectful, and listen to every person's point of view.
◆ Members may have a lot to contribute but are held back because of a closed relationship with each member.	◆ Members are encouraged to offer their skills and knowledge, and in turn each member is able contribute to the group's success.
◆ Members are bothered by differing opinions or disagreements because they consider it a threat. There is not group support to help resolve problems.	◆ Members see conflict as a part of human nature and they react to it by treating it as an opportunity to hear about new ideas and opinions. Everybody wants to resolve problems constructively.

their classroom, that they aren't working in isolation, and that everyone works together. The highest performing schools have teachers who understand that these are all our kids (not just "the ones I teach"), and that we are in this together. When it is the "I" mentality and not the "team" mentality, teachers don't see faculty meetings as important, they don't see giving input for decisions to be necessary, and they may feel like they are competing against other teachers. This is not a healthy environment to bring out the best in all teachers.

 Pause to Reflect: Do some teams in your school essentially function more like a group? How can they be a true team?

Why Do Teams Matter?

As mentioned earlier, principals also have one of the toughest jobs in America, with an average turnover rate turn every three years, and more frequently in high-needs schools, according to School Leaders Network (2014). With a full plate and a myriad of issues to tackle, leaders have a full plate that is all but impossible tackle alone. So when it comes to team building, not only are you putting teachers first, but you are also making your own job easier in the process.

In their five-year study of 180 schools, a team of researchers found that nearly all of the staff working in high-performing schools had more influence over school decisions than did staff from low-performing schools (Seashore, Leithwood, & Anderson, 2010). Their research indicated that collective leadership, if organized and managed effectively, has a greater impact on outcomes than any one individual can. This means if you are willing to trust your teachers with more responsibility, autonomy, and freedom, you can create a winning team. High-performing schools aren't built on only the work of a good leader, but on the work of a great team led by a great administration!

You may be thinking that you already have teams. For instance, we make use of grade-level teams such as a fifth-grade team. This grouping defines the team (everyone teaches the same grade), but it doesn't necessarily explain why it exists. A purpose for being a grade-level team could be, "We are a team of teachers who support each other, share ideas, learn from each other, and identify ways that we can better meet the needs of our fifth-grade students." It's important to be clear on a team's purpose and goals. And consider adding vertical teams, not just grade-level ones. Vertical teams are not content or grade specific but schoolwide in nature. Examples of vertical teams include school-wide leadership teams and curriculum teams and will be discussed in more detail later in the chapter. It may take a little time and effort to create these teams, but it is worth the effort. Cohesive teams build unity, nurture relationships, increase job satisfaction, and provide a means for mentoring and supporting teachers and administrators. First, let's look at all of the reasons that teams matter.

1. Teams Build Unity

A cohesive team promotes an atmosphere that nurtures friendship and loyalty. These close-knit relationships motivate employees to work harder, cooperate, and be supportive of one another. Individuals possess diverse strengths, weaknesses, communication skills, and habits. Therefore, when a teamwork environment is not encouraged, this can pose many challenges toward achieving the overall goals and objectives. This creates an environment where employees become focused on promoting their own achievements.

One area that is often not addressed is the competition that exists between some teachers when there isn't a true team concept. Teachers will compete with each other (to have better looking rooms, to have better lessons/units, to have parents like them more), and it seems to stem from the lack of appreciation they receive from their administration. When teachers don't get that acknowledgement or don't feel valued, they will begin to compete with their peers, subconsciously or not, for that attention. The team concept helps build unity, where teachers realize they aren't in competition with each other, but that they are there to make each other better. Unity creates value for all the members.

2. Teams Allow for the Sharing of Resources and Expertise

Teams enable teachers to work with their peers and focus on improvement rather than evaluation. When teachers work together in teams, they coach each other, learn from one another, and share their expertise in specific areas. This cohesive dynamic—in which everyone plays a role and is valued—provides them with a safe space to refine their practices to improve student outcomes. It also boosts teacher morale, making it more likely that good teachers will stay in the profession longer. In these collaborative environments, all teachers improve because they get the best from each other.

In addition, individuals can expand their skill sets and discover fresh ideas from colleagues. For example, if a teacher has great lessons for improving writing, or a science teacher has labs that the students love, those should be shared among the staff, not kept in isolation in one classroom. While the focus here is on teachers and team building, students are the ultimate winners, of course.

3. Teams Allow for Greater Efficiency

The story is told of a team of about 35 teachers that had come together for a team-building event. They were a young, bright, and enthusiastic team. However, one big problem this team had was they wouldn't share information or solutions with each other. The leader felt they were too focused on themselves and not enough on being a team. So she started off with a fun team activity that would allow her to teach the importance of each team member working together and sharing more.

She brought the team into the cafeteria. All of the tables and chairs had been stacked and put away. Placed around the room were fun decorations and hundreds of different colored balloons. Everyone was excited by the setup but unsure what was happening. In the center of the room was a big box of balloons that had not been blown up yet. The team leader asked each person to pick a balloon, blow it up and write their name on it. But they were instructed to be careful because the balloon could pop!

A few balloons did indeed pop and those members of the team were given another chance, but were told that if the balloon popped again they were out of the game. About 30 team members were able to get their name on a balloon without it popping. Those 30 were asked to leave their balloons and exit the room. They were told they had qualified for the second round.

Five minutes later the leader brought the team back into the room and announced that their next challenge was to find the balloon they had left behind with their name on it among the hundreds of other balloons scattered in the large cafeteria. She warned them, however, to be very careful and not to pop any of the balloons. If they did, they would be disqualified.

While being very careful, but also trying to go as quickly as they could, each team member looked for the balloon with his or her name. After 15 minutes, not one single person was able to find his or her balloon. The team was told that the second round of the game was over and they were moving onto the third round.

In this next round, the leader told the team members to find any balloon in the room with a name on it and give it to the person whose name was on it. Within a couple of minutes every member of the team had their balloon with their own name on it.

The team leader made the following point: "We are much more efficient when we are willing to share with each other. And we are better problem solvers when we are working together, not individually."

While this is a great example of how teamwork can improve efficiency, it is important to note that much more complex processes can be made easier as well. This is because it allows the workload to be shared, reduce the pressure on individuals, and ensure tasks are completed on time. It also allows goals to be more attainable, enhances the optimization of performance, improves job satisfaction, and decreases workload. Teamwork allows us to streamline responsibilities, communicate more efficiently, and produce higher quality work in a shorter time period.

4. Teams Provide Support for Teachers

Teaching has historically been viewed as an isolated profession. Even the teachers' lounge has become more of a place to grab a snack, or check your mail box. It has not been a place to collaborate, or spend time developing relationships, there just simply isn't the time. Because of this mindset, teachers often feel like they are in it alone and when things aren't going well, they don't feel like they have anywhere to turn. However, with cohesive teams, **teachers should have a great support system of** peers/colleagues/administrators. For example, when teachers receive negative specific feedback, they feel isolated. They are not sure who to go to or they may not want others to help because they're embarrassed. That's why it's important to have teams where they feel support and encouragement. It's also important for administrators to know teachers' needs and strengths, so they can provide support or have other teachers provide support. It's great when teams are high achieving, but the members of the team shouldn't be competitive or trying to undermine other team members.

Support builds morale within a team. You'll feel that your work is valued when you contribute to something that produces results. If you offer an idea that helps improve productivity, such as a new online communication system, confidence and trust is built within the team. Each team member has something unique to offer. By working together, members of a team feel a strong sense of belonging and deep commitment to each other and their common goals.

Team members want to work together for the good of the team and understand that combining the skills of numerous people will produce something that could not be created alone. The strengths of each team member are being utilized.

Keys to a Cohesive Team

While creating teams make take a little effort, doing so will change the culture of the school. It will increase unity among the staff, and it will make tasks more efficient and effective. Moving from an average or low-performing school to a high-performing school can be accomplished without a radical change in faculty, but it does require a radical change in how your faculty is viewed and utilized. If you want to see your teachers really shine and your school standout, then make the cohesive team a priority. A cohesive school team is unified while working toward a goal and while also satisfying the emotional needs of its members.

Think of it from a sports perspective. Some of the greatest teams in history won consistently because they had a cohesive team. These teams may have had one or two superstars, but they won consistently because of their role players. The coaches knew how to maximize the strengths of the average players. These role players are the average players who perform consistently on a daily basis. They aren't superstars, but they are good and they are dependable. And the coaches know that when they put the right people in the right roles and give them the tools necessary to do their job, success is all but guaranteed. So it's not about having a school full of superstars, but about maximizing the potential of the faculty you have. An important note here is that even your introverted teachers still have strengths and abilities, so the key is to place them where their strengths can be utilized. This makes it less about personality and more about what they bring to the team, so they will tend to be more comfortable and perform better. **Remember even the greatest superstar needs teammates to make a great team.**

Babe Ruth once said, "The way a team plays as a whole determines its success. You may have the greatest bunch of individual stars in the world, but if they don't play together, the club won't be worth a dime" (Tredgold, 2016) As an administrator, you may have one or two superstars on your team, and if you're lucky maybe even three or four, but you don't have a team full of them. So, build a great team by getting the best out of every teacher, not just the superstar, but everyone. Take the time to place teachers in the best position for them to succeed. This will ensure that your teams are working together like a cohesive unit.

Here are some other keys to a great team.

1. Inspire Team Leadership

In leadership, the irony is that it's not about you, but it's all about you. It's not about you in the sense that the successes and achievements shouldn't be about you, but about your team. But it is about you because you are the one who creates the environment for your team to be successful. We have all heard about getting everyone in the right seat on the bus, but what if the bus is going in the wrong direction, or worse, off a cliff? Does it matter who sits where in that scenario? Hardly. So putting together the best team(s), developing leaders within the teams, and creating a climate where everyone can succeed is largely on the administration.

The team's leader is ultimately responsible for setting the tone. The leader never stops leading, coaching, and teaching. He or she keeps a fresh perspective and is always challenging the team to think differently. You know that you have solid team leaders when they are 100% focused on the team and not on themselves. Teachers appreciate leaders who are actively involved in supporting team efforts by getting their hands dirty along the way. The leaders often set the tone for interaction and are the catalyst for improvement. Mutual respect and camaraderie are two of the most critical factors contributing to a leader's success.

2. Have a Clear Vision

Every team should have a clear vision or purpose. It's not enough to say, "We're the sixth grade team of teachers." A purpose for being a team might be: "We come together as a team to support each other, learn from each other, and identify ways we can better meet the needs of our sixth grade students." The purpose should be relevant, meaningful, and clear. It should not be just to hold more meetings or to check off some box about serving on a committee.

Here are some key traits of a clear mission, based on the book *The Five Dysfunctions of a Team* (Lencioni, 2002).

- ◆ There are clearly defined, transparent goals aligned with the mission of the district.
- ◆ All team members are committed to these goals and to a clearly articulated plan of action.
- ◆ Goals are specific, measurable, attainable, realistic, and timely (SMART).
- ◆ There is shared clarity about how the work of the team will affect student achievement.

3. Build Trust

Team members don't have to be best friends, but they do have to build a level of trust to be effective. There needs to be trust in leadership, in teammates, and even in the established process. Teachers could grow complacent or frustrated if they don't feel their strengths are being utilized or their voices are being heard. Even when there is conflict, which is all but inevitable, it should be managed. There need to be agreements about how we treat each other and engage with each other. There also needs to be someone, such as a facilitator, who ensures that this is a safe space. Furthermore, in order for there to be trust within a strong team, we see equitable participation amongst members and shared decision-making. Respect is an important part of trust, because we value what each person brings to the team. Here are some key components to developing trust, based on *The Five Dysfunctions of a Team* (Lencioni, 2002). When you trust, you:

- ◆ Are able to engage in "unfiltered conflict" around ideas.
- ◆ Admit weaknesses and mistakes and ask for help.
- ◆ Accept questions and input about their areas of responsibility.
- ◆ Give one another the benefit of the doubt before arriving at a negative conclusion.
- ◆ Take risks in offering feedback and assistance.
- ◆ Appreciate and tap into one another's skills and experiences.
- ◆ Offer and accept apologies without hesitation.

4. Create Vertical Teams

When we think of teams, horizontal ones (such as grade-level teams) usually come to mind. These teams are important because they help teachers focus on best teaching and learning practices. Vertical teams are not as common in most schools, but they are visible in high-performing schools. They require a little more work to create but can be well worth it. The key is to ensure group members bring the right skills to the table and understand their job function. Underperforming teams often don't have the right skills they need to get the job done. Make sure your vertical teams have individuals with varying strengths to bring balance, such as an analytical person, creative person, etc. The teams that know how to work together and divvy up project tasks gain the most from their group's unique mix of knowledge and abilities. You may have some vertical teams in place, such as a leadership or curriculum team, but there are many potential teams that could help you create a high0performing school.

According to an article in *The Balance* by Susan Heathfield (2016), there are five vertical teams which are important to most organizations.

◆ **The leadership team** can include all administrators as well as department heads, and others that you feel bring strengths to the team. The leadership team is the group that strategically leads your school.

◆ **The motivation or morale team** plans and carries out events and activities that build a positive spirit among employees. The team's responsibilities can include activities such as hosting lunches, planning picnics, fundraising for ill employees, etc.

◆ **The safety or environmental team** takes the lead in safety training, monthly safety talks, and the auditing of housekeeping, safety, and workplace organization. Recycling or even "going green" environmental policy recommendations are provided by the team as well.

◆ **The culture or communication team** works to define and create the defined company culture necessary for the success of your organization. The team also fosters two-way communication in your organization to ensure employee input up the chain of command. The team may sponsor the monthly newsletter, a weekly company update, quarterly employee satisfaction surveys, and an employee suggestion process.

◆ **The teacher wellness team** focuses on health and fitness for employees. Most popular activities include walking clubs, running teams, and periodic testing of health issues such as high blood pressure screenings. This team could set up events, such as a walking challenge to encourage faculty to get moving more. Each participant could be given a pedometer to be downloaded daily at work. At the end of the challenge, there could be prizes for top performers.

 Pause to Reflect: What are a few ways you will improve the teams in your school and/or add on new, vertical teams?

Flawless Team Execution

Flawless execution isn't about being perfect, but about preparing and executing the best game plan possible. Flawless execution occurs when every member is in the zone, working in unison with one another, and when they have each other's backs. Great teams don't need to be taught how to be a great team, but they simply need to be reminded about the things they must keep doing to succeed. Here are some things all teams need to keep in mind:

1. Make a Game Plan Together

When creating goals and objectives, every team member needs to be part of the process. Set Clear Goals. Ask the questions: what is our purpose? What do we plan to achieve? This is necessary so that all team members understand the purpose and vision of the team. It is important to understand where the team is headed. People tend to support what they help to create. Team members who are involved in establishing the goals will work harder to achieve them.

When creating your game plan, keep the SMART (Rubin, 2002) goals in mind:

- ◆ **S**pecific (simple, sensible, significant)
- ◆ **M**easurable (meaningful, motivating)
- ◆ **A**chievable (agreed, attainable)
- ◆ **R**elevant (reasonable, realistic and resourced, results-based)
- ◆ **T**ime bound (time-based, time limited, time/cost limited, timely, time-sensitive).

2. Clearly Define Roles and Responsibilities

Begin by establishing leadership in the group. The leader doesn't necessarily have to be an administrator. In fact, you don't even need one person; you can have a rotation of people who steer the ship. But having the leadership established early on ensures that there is the intentionality, planning, and facilitation that is essential for a team to be high functioning.

The leader or leaders can then more effectively and clearly define the roles and responsibilities of those on the team. Don't assume this is an easy step; in fact, you'll often find that people's ideal roles lie outside their job descriptions. It may be their strengths rather than their position that benefits the team.

Each of your team member's responsibilities must be interconnected and dependent upon one another. This is not unlike team sports, where some of your role players can make a big impact. Remember they may not be the most talented person on the team, but they know how to work best within the system. This is why you must have a keen eye for talent and be able to evaluate people not only on their ability to play a particular role, but even more so on whether they fit the workplace culture (the system) and will be a team player.

If you are the leader of the group, then don't try to do everything yourself. As leader, it is your role to set objectives and make sure the right outcomes are achieved, but let the team know they are responsible for achieving the goals and that they are accountable. Remember not to micromanage, because people do things in many different ways and more often than not their way of doing them may be the better way. So just keep them accountable and if issues arise, then the team can focus on the issues.

3. Hold Everyone Accountable to the Team

Whether your team members are the superstars or role players, they are equally important. The best teams are those where each member on the team is accountable to themselves and to each other. They are clear about their role and responsibilities. Peer pressure is a powerful force, particularly when people are working with those whom they respect and don't want to let down.

The desire to perform well and help teachers team succeed can also override the dips in motivation that you encounter on days when they're not at your best. And remember that accountability is multi-directional. This means the leader is as accountable to the team as the team is to the leader. This is an important concept to remember in any leadership role.

Here are a few ideas to keep in mind when it comes to team accountability.

- ◆ Hold one another accountable and feel a sense of obligation to the team for progress.
- ◆ Review, study, interpret, and act on data.
- ◆ Willingly review progress, be able to describe the work to others, and welcome feedback and suggestions.
- ◆ Identify potential problems quickly by questioning one another's approaches without hesitation.
- ◆ Routinely monitor progress on SMART goals.

4. Embrace Conflict

Discussions can nurture deep professional learning as individuals and teams explore new ideas for practice. However, they may also lead to conflict, especially when you have individuals with different strengths, perspectives, and experiences. Conflict, however, is not necessarily bad, as discussed in the communication chapter. In fact, team conflict can sometimes create better solutions. Of course, we don't want people who have to argue with every idea just for the sake of argument, but if something doesn't seem as logical as it sounds, maybe there does need to be more discussion.

5. Celebrate Your Teammates

Take the time to give your teammates the proper accolades they have earned and deserve. Some leaders take performance for granted because they don't believe that one should be rewarded for "doing their job." But celebrating successes and milestones brings a team together and allows everyone to see that when they work together, great things can happen. If someone does a great job at something, give them a shout out in front of the rest of the team so that every effort is seen and appreciated. This also helps each person to feel visible and that what they're doing has an impact. In contrast, if your team fails at something, come together to redirect your efforts or turn it into something positive. Don't throw anyone under the bus or turn a damage-control discussion into a blame game. This never helps anybody. Instead, give your team equal responsibility to put your heads together and figure out the next steps. Remember there will be mistakes and failures, but with the support of the team, the focus is on always improving, on greater success, and on creating a higher performing school.

As we leave this chapter, remember that great accomplishments can be achieved through teams. The role of a teacher is like a player on a sport team: all teachers are vital on their own, but the chemistry or culture of the school is even more important for the overall quality of the school. Pro and Olympic sports offer numerous examples of teams that have performed beyond expectations because of leadership, commitment, and team chemistry. Perhaps you have heard of the "Miracle on Ice" US ice hockey team, when a team of college kids beat both Soviet and Finland in the final rounds to win the gold medal in the 1980 Winter Olympics. The quality of Team USA certainly exceeded the quality of its players. That can be true in education, too. Never overlook the importance of your team.

Chapter 8: Key Points to Remember

- **Creating teams allows your faculty to utilize their strengths**. Remember these are random groups of people, but choose people who will fit and benefit the team.
- **Remember role players are as important as the superstar.** Not everyone is a superstar nor does everyone need to be. Every teacher has special strengths they bring to the team and without them there is no real team chemistry. And everyone is important!
- **Include teachers on vertical teams as well.** Vertical teams are less common than horizontal ones but are also

important. Remember your teachers have more strengths and expertise than just as a classroom teacher. You have invaluable resources in your teachers, so use them.

◆ **Teams offer an opportunity for unity and support.** Remember that teaching can seem very isolating, and teams give teachers a sense of common purpose and support. They need people with whom to bounce ideas off, as well as someone with whom they can share problems. Teachers like the "we are all in this together" concept.

◆ **Give teachers responsibility on teams**. One of the best ways to treat teachers like adults is to let them be adults. Adults have responsibilities and they have decision-making power with those responsibilities. Don't micromanage; trust your teams to make the best decisions for the school.

◆ **Team conflict can actually lead to better practices or improved results.** This concept is worth repeating throughout the book because conflict is often seen as a negative and divisive to teams. But the reality is you have people on your teams with different strengths, perspectives, and expertise, so some may identify issues that others don't see.

◆ **Focus on flawless execution.** This doesn't mean the team or individuals are going to be perfect, but it's about improving performance over time. Even professional teams spend a lot of time focused on improving performance, so they will be more effective in game situations.

◆ **Celebrate team successes.** What does a sports team do immediately after they win a championship? They celebrate. Don't be afraid to celebrate your team and with your team!

9

Celebrating Successes

When people enter your school, they should immediately sense how it is different from other schools. They should see staff members smiling and feel enjoyment in the air. The research that has been presented is clear: when you put teachers first, it creates a high-performing culture. Teachers who are recognized and appreciated will typically see better academic results when compared to teachers who do not feel appreciated. Remember the Gallup research shows that when employees feel recognized and valued, and feel that their strengths are utilized, they are six times more productive, more engaged, and feel like they have a higher quality of life (Flade, Asplund, & Elliot, 2015). This is how high-performing schools are created and when students have the greatest opportunity to maximize their achievement.

Every administrator should want a building full of happy and engaged teachers. It is imperative that administrators recognize the value of keeping teacher morale high. Morale isn't kept at an optimal level if you wait until the end of the year to recognize or celebrate teachers. When it's only emphasized for a day or week, then that's when we know morale is more than likely lousy.

Why Celebrate Teachers?

It's interesting that we celebrate musicians, athletes, and Hollywood stars, because we think they're talented, they influence pop culture, and we can relate to them on some level because of their contributions. Ironically, many if not all of them would not be where they are without the encouragement and belief of some teacher (remember Walt Disney's teacher?). But teachers themselves are rarely given the adulation they deserve when it comes to their talent and influence on others.

As an educational leader, you have the capacity to build morale by creating a positive work environment. Make teachers feel valued by praising their accomplishments. There are many reasons to celebrate teachers, and here a few key ones:

1. Everyone Wants and Needs to Be Appreciated

Wanting to feel appreciated is a core emotional need for all humans. We all like to feel like what we do matters, that it is appreciated, and that we are appreciated. It's part of our human make-up. A simple verbal thank you, a handwritten note, or a pat on the back can incentivize your teachers to work harder. Celebrating small wins as a team enhances morale; it helps teams maintain focus on what they're working toward while giving everyone a chance to reflect on their successes.

2. Teachers Work So Hard

If someone who sings or can score a touchdown is so easily celebrated, then celebrating teachers should be a no brainer. Teachers are some of the hardest workers out there. Anyone who can get up every day to meet the needs and accommodate learning styles of 30 students per class, deal with parents, prepare lessons, grade tests, all while inspiring the uninspired, loving the unlovable, and at times, teaching the unteachable deserves to be celebrated every day!

3. Teachers Are Difference Makers

No other professionals so greatly influence others as teachers do. Just about everyone can point to one or more teachers who have had an impact on their lives. We may not even realize it at the time, but looking back, we can see how certain teachers shaped our thoughts and helped us to achieve far more than we could ever have imagined. They teach us to believe in ourselves and to never say "I can't." Teachers influence the present and the future.

Cheerleaders Lead the Celebration of the school

The school leader has to be a cheerleader for the school faculty. Be that cheerleader for your staff, encourage them, celebrate victories, and use the megaphone for jobs well done. The value of this role should not be underestimated. Recent research by Dr. Shelly Gable (UCLA) showed that a person who responds enthusiastically—like a cheerleader—to good news produces a stronger and healthier relationship than a person who responds compassionately to bad news (Gable, 2007).

The cheerleader focuses on their teachers' strengths. Being intentional about calling out someone's strengths is essential to being a cheerleader. Being a cheerleader creates an environment where people feel safe to dream and take risks. It produces more innovation and outside the box thinking. So when your teachers do something wonderful, make sure you immediately give an energetic and constructive response. On the other hand, when your teachers hit roadblocks or make mistakes at work, the cheer-leader will act understanding, resists the temptation to add insult to injury, and makes sure they move past it. It's okay for teachers to make mistakes, but help them reflect and move past them.

Cheerleaders rise to the occasion for the following:

- ◆ Positive events
- ◆ Victories
- ◆ A job well done

♦ Empathetic to employees who experience a setback, bad news, or mistake

---

 Pause to Reflect: Are you as enthusiastic about good news as you are serious or upset about bad news? How can you show more cheer when things go well?

Keys to Effective Recognition and Praise

Recognition is an important key to teacher success. As Dr. Diane Hodges, author of *Looking Forward to Monday Morning*, explains, "No one gets up in the morning and says, "I think I will just be mediocre today." People want to do a good job, and given the proper environment and encouragement, they will," she writes. "The strongest motivators are not monetary rewards or benefits. People want to be appreciated for what they do. And when their supervisor and colleagues give recognition and appreciation on their behalf, people do their best" (Hodges, 2013). Now this doesn't mean that you should be recognizing or rewarding everything your teachers do. Showing up on time isn't really something to celebrate, but an expectation. But when you implement the strategies we have suggested and focus on teacher strengths, you will find many genuine opportunities to recognize and celebrate your teachers.

Recognition isn't just about feeling good. As we mentioned earlier, keep in mind that teachers who receive regular recognition and praise might be:

♦ more productive
♦ more engaged at work
♦ more likely to stay with their school
♦ more likely to receive higher satisfaction scores from students and parents.

So exactly how do you recognize teachers in the most effective manner? Here are a few ways.

1. Make Recognition Timely

Recognition is a powerful, positive way to reinforce action or behaviors you want to see again and again, but that power is diluted the longer you wait to recognize someone. Make sure you share your detailed, specific praise soon after the event worthy of recognition. For instance, if you observe a teacher delivering an amazing lesson, don't wait until the end of the day or week to let her know. Leave her a note as you leave the room, send her an email as soon as you get back to your office, or even verbally praise her in class as you leave. Recognizing great work is not disruptive to the learning process, but is an important part of it.

2. Be Specific

There isn't much more wasteful or in some ways insulting than giving generic praise. "You did a great job in class today!" What does that mean? What did they do great? Be detailed in what they did that was great! Compliments that are too generic tend to seem insincere. The more specific you can be, the more likely it is to be repeated. Also, don't cloud it with anything extra. Remember the "leave the buts behind" recommendation in the appreciation chapter.

3. Be Sincere

You also need to be sincere. All praise must be based on a true appreciation of, and excitement about, the other person's success. Otherwise your thanks may come across as manipulative rather than genuine. You should want your faculty to succeed exceedingly. Make it meaningful as well. If you hand write a note to a teacher, then they know it's not just you checking off the box that you recognized them, but that you are sincere and value them. Some teachers will keep these handwritten notes stashed and pull them out in a bad day, and get reenergized because they remember you are there for them!

4. Make It Frequent

Recognition should never be viewed as a "one-and-done" task or something you put on your calendar to do on a monthly basis. Just as recognition should be timely, it should also occur every time you see exceptional behaviors, actions, or outcomes. Remember the CEO who kept pennies in his pocket to remind him to say a certain number of positive things each day? Use pennies or whatever it takes to get in the habit of praising of your teachers.

5. Acknowledge Individuals

Each of your teachers has unique set of personality traits and strengths. Some may thrive by working independently (sans micromanaging) while others may need constant reassurance that they're doing a good job. By remembering there's no "one size fits all" when it comes to motivating and improving teacher morale, you can garner better results. When you lead based upon only your preferred work style, you risk mismanaging people who have different strengths and need different levels of support from you. Make sure you're adapting your style to fit their needs. Even if you have introverted teachers, you will know how to best recognize them and let them know they are valued. If you want to give a physical token of appreciation to a particular team member, make sure it's unique and meaningful.

6. Focus on Team Effort

Teachers notice the great things their colleagues do for their students, so ask them to share that with you. If you've already built a culture of positivity through your willingness to openly praise your staff, they'll follow your lead. Or better yet, create a vertical team that focuses on things like morale, appreciation, and celebration.

7. Recognize Effort, Not Just Results

We are used to rewarding results. If someone achieves a goal, then we reward it. However, if we truly value innovation and curiosity, then we have to recognize *effort* as well. We know that not everything a teacher tries will be successful, but this doesn't mean that the effort shouldn't be recognized. In fact, when we focus on accountability or results, then we lose sight of innovation and outside the box thinking, which are the traits we hope to instill in our students, not just our teachers. When teachers try challenging or innovative things, they may not meet our expectations, but the willingness to take risks still needs to be recognized for the effort shown.

 Pause to Reflect: Think of one or two teachers whom you can recognize this week. How will you go about it?

Great Ideas to Celebrate Teachers

While it's great to offer praise and recognition to teachers, don't forget the little incentives and rewards for a job well done. The beauty of having a school community and extended community is that most people are vested in the schools and will often provide support for your celebration ideas. If you are not great at reaching out to these groups, then this would be a great opportunity to create a vertical team that focuses on celebrations. Here are a variety of ideas that you can use to make your teachers feel like they are superstars and know you put them first!

- ◆ Provide coffee regularly for teachers. Enlist the help of the PTO, homeroom parents, and local companies to alternate sponsoring one morning each week. This can also work for lunches as well. It's also a great way to connect with the community and let them put teachers first as well.
- ◆ Make your school warm and inviting with little touches for a cozy and creative atmosphere. Add plants or flowers in the front office and teachers' lounge. Provide healthy snacks in the teachers' lounge. "Research has shown that the environment can be more important and more motivating than money," explains Dr. Nicole Lipkin, organizational psychologist and CEO of Equilibria Leadership Consulting. "When your surroundings are inspiring, your brain is more likely to be inspiring too" (Rosenthal, 2017).

- ◆ If you live in an area where snow is common, scrape or brush off teachers' cars so they can get on the road soon after the bell rings. Allow students to help if age appropriate, such as through an honor's club. If you do not live in an area where it snows often, perhaps you could bring in a local company to wash teachers' car once or twice a year. For the publicity and potential business, the company might do this without charging a cent!

- ◆ Keep a note pad with you at all times. When you see something inspirational in a classroom, write a note of praise for the teacher and leave it on the desk. If no one is in a room you enter, leave a note on the board expressing how lucky the students are to have their teacher. One principal shared that in the quiet hours before the school's open house, she took the time to leave a brief post-it note of thanks and inspiration on each teacher's desk.

- ◆ Give away a Two-Hour Break. At each faculty meeting, hold a lottery drawing for a "free" two-hour break during which time you will cover a teacher's class. Let the winner know that s/he can use this ticket at any time, but must set the time a week in advance.

- ◆ Deliver a PA Announcement. Remember Mega Mike? He used the ship public address system to give shout outs to his crew. Makes use of your PA system for more than morning announcements or to call students to the office. For example, "A big thank you to Mr. Williams and Mrs. Simons for staying after the concert last night and helping to put away chairs." Not only would such an announcement make the teachers feel good, but it would show students what the school values.

- ◆ Make a strong connection with the local news outlet. Whether it is radio, television, or newspaper, they can report on things happening within the school, outside projects that teachers do, or other events. Showcase your teachers and school as often as possible to the community.

- ◆ Professional Development Day of Rest. . . . Many schools have built in PD Days throughout the year. Take one of these PD days and let your teachers use the day to do whatever they want—go shopping, out to lunch, or to the spa. Just don't let them use it at school working. Your teachers will appreciate you beyond words!

◆ And while we want praise and even celebration to be continuous, it's okay to go all out during a week of teacher appreciation. Make each day theme-related or simply provide a different treat each day. Pick one item for each day of the week. Ideas can include breakfast one morning, lunch one day, shoulder massages at lunch, and maybe even an ice cream social immediately after school along with an awards celebration.

 Pause to Reflect: Aside from giving individual recognition, what is a bigger idea you can try from this chapter for celebrating all of the teachers on your staff?

Celebrate Health, Too

In a profession that can be overtly sedentary and highly stressful, one of the best ways to put your teachers first is to focus on their health. The beauty of getting your faculty physically active is that it not only reduces stress but will give them more energy, make them feel better, and improve their overall physical fitness. And there are noted benefits of employees who are healthy. Research from the Health Enhancement Research Organization (HERO), Brigham Young University, and the Center for Health Research at Healthways shows

◆ Employees who eat healthy all day long were 25% more likely to have higher job performance.
◆ Employees who exercise for at least 30 minutes, three times a week, were 15% more likely to have higher job performance.
◆ Absenteeism was 27% lower for those workers who ate healthy and regularly exercised (Brooks, 2013).

So how can you encourage and celebrate health? Provide opportunities for teachers to be active or invite fitness experts in to discuss proper nutrition or to provide different exercise options for the teachers. Make classrooms more active by incorporating more physical activity in content areas (Johnson, 2017). Below are a few more ideas to help you celebrate teachers' health.

- ◆ Encourage teachers to make learning more active, so they are up moving with the kids throughout the day. This can include giving teachers a pedometer so they can track their miles. Give awards or prizes for top performers.
- ◆ Treat teachers to a massage. Hire a professional to set up in the teacher's lounge and offer 5-minute massages during breaks and lunch. Better yet, ask them to donate their time to the school or share the cost with the PTO.
- ◆ Set up a lunchroom schedule so teachers can take a 15-minute walk just to burn off some energy or recharge. This can be done by having parent volunteers work in the lunchroom instead of teachers, or by having more administration supervision during that time to allow more teachers the opportunity to participate.
- ◆ If you have a teacher who has a fitness passion, like yoga or Zumba, let them offer classes after or before school. It's even better if the school can pay the teacher for her time.
- ◆ Encourage teachers to have a small fridge in the classroom to keep water, healthy foods, and snacks, etc. Remember teachers don't have the freedom to leave the building at any time, so this gives them the opportunity to make healthy choices.

Remember that teachers are humans and that education is a social endeavor. So, recognize the great work your teachers do, and do not be afraid to celebrate their successes and their innovation. High-performing schools don't just randomly occur, but they are built by a strong administration, who understands that when they put teachers first, they will put students first. So motivate, encourage, appreciate, and most of all celebrate them! They are the caretakers of the next generation!

Chapter 9: Key Points to Remember

- **Small successes are important too.** There are no small victories, especially when it comes to successes in school. So, don't be afraid to acknowledge and celebrate the little things. Remember the words of Rachael Robertson? The little moments build momentum!

- **Say Thank You.** . . . If you are married, do you tell your spouse that you appreciate them and thank them only occasionally? Or say I just told them thanks a couple of months ago? No, you do it often. Or at least you should be, if you want a thriving relationship. The same is true of professional relationships, too. Let them know you appreciate all that they do.

- **Teachers with higher morale are more productive**. When teachers feel recognized and celebrated, they can be up to six times more productive. Isn't that a teacher that you want in the classroom? Yes!

- **Helps teachers manage stress.** It's hard to feel your best or give your best when you are stressed out. Provide opportunities for teachers to participate in fitness activities at school, in the classroom, and provide healthy snacks for them when possible.

- **Celebrate often!** Make celebrating a common occurrence, not a one and done. And don't wait until teacher appreciation week.

- **Finally, Never, Never, Never forget the importance of teaching**. Our teachers are the caretakers of each generation of learners. They impact lives today and for the future. So don't forget to take care of the caretakers! Put teachers first!

Final Thought

Finally, remember that teaching is the noblest of all professions and that teachers not only affect the lives of their students, but the legacy they leave can influence generations to come.

To illustrate this point, we have to look no further than another one of my cousins, Tammy Layne Waddell. Tammy was a teacher for over 25 years. She taught special education and regular education classes at various times throughout her career. Regardless of the class of grade level, one thing was always true, she loved her students, and they loved her. Whether it was a hug or school supplies, she always had what the students needed. She always made sure they were having a good day, even if it was just in her class.

Sadly, Tammy recently passed away, but her story does not end there. Her last request, when she was faced with her mortality, was for friends and family to bring backpacks full of supplies to her funeral instead of flowers. She was always thinking of others first and said there were many students in need within the community. At the funeral, there were over 100 backpacks lined along the chapel pews and up front. About 50 teachers were honorary pallbearers and after the service, they formed a long line for the casket to be carried through to the hearse.

A picture of the backpacks sitting by the pews in an empty chapel was posted on Twitter and it went viral, reaching millions of people worldwide! Every major media outlet (CNN, FOX, MSN, ABC, NBC, CBS) called, messaged, or texted for me to share with them about my cousin and her final act of compassion. A teacher who lived in relative anonymity in the world became a source of inspiration to the world with her final lesson which was to put students first.

Well, Tammy definitely put her fingerprints on her work, she swam in the deep end and she did something big. By putting your teachers first, you allow them to do what they do best, which is to not only inspire students but quite possibly the whole world.

References

Akers, M., & Porter, G. (2003). Your EQ Skills: Got What it Takes? *Journal of Accountancy* Vol. 195, No. 3, pp. 65–69.

Amabile, T. (2011). *The Progress Principle: Using Small Wins to Ignite Joy, Engagement, and Creativity at Work*. Boston, MA: Harvard Business Review Press.

Barrier, M. (2007). *The Animated Man: A Life of Walt Disney*. Berkeley: University of California Press.

Barsade, Sig (2002). The Ripple Effect: Emotional Contagion and Its Influence on Group Behavior. *Administrative Science Quarterly* Vol. 47, No. 4, pp. 644–675.

Billington, Anne (2017, October 16). Personal Interview.

Booth, B. (2016). 5 Tips to Become an Authentic Leader. *Kellogg Insight*. Retrieved from https://insight.kellogg.northwestern.edu/article/five-tips-for-authentic-leadership

Booher, Dianna (2017, December). Personal Interview.

Bradberry, Travis (2009). *Emotional Intelligence 2.0*. San Diego: Talent Smart.

Brooks, Chad (2013). You Are What You Eat . . . Even at Work. *Business News Daily*. Retrieved from www.businessnewsdaily.com/3699-healthy-eating-worker-productivity.html

Broussard, M. (2014). Why Poor Schools Can't Win at Standardized Testing. *The Atlantic*. Retrieved from www.theatlantic.com/education/archive/2014/07/why-poor-schools-cant-win-at-standardized-testing/374287/

Chueng, R. (2015). Why Hong Kong School Principals Need High EQ to Cope with Change. *South China Morning Post*. Retrieved www.scmp.com/lifestyle/families/article/1840901/why-hong-kong-school-principals-need-high-eq-cope-change

Cleaver, S. (2013). Teach to Your Strengths. *We Are Teachers*. Retrieved from www.weareteachers.com/teach-to-your-strengths/

Collins, Jim (2011). *Great by Choice: Uncertainty, Chaos, and Luck-Why Some Thrive Despite Them All*. New York: Harper Business.

Covey, S. (2004). *The 7 Habits of Highly Effective People: Powerful Lessons in Personal Change*. New York: Free Press.

Crouch, D. (2015). Highly Trained, Respected and Free: Why Finland's Teachers are Different. *The Guardian*. Retrieved from www.theguardian.com/education/2015/jun/17/highly-trained-respected-and-free-why-finlands-teachers-are-different

Currie, Brad (2017, November 12). Personal interview.

Damasio, A. (2005). *Descartes' Error: Emotion, Reason, and the Human Brain*. New York: Penguin Books.

Danks, Teresa (2017, December 15). Personal interview.

Demirtas, Z. (2010). Teachers' Job Satisfaction Levels. *Procedia-Social and Behavioral Sciences* Vol. 9, pp. 1069–1073.

Disney, Walt (1955). Interview with Journal of California Teachers Association. Retrieved from www.mouseplanet.com/8210/Walts_Favorite_Teacher_Daisy_Beck

Dyer, Wayne quote. Retrieved from http://quozio.com/quote/69b9b524#!t=1000

Elton, Chester (2009). *The Carrot Principle: How the Best Managers Use Recognition to Engage Their People, Retain Talent, and Accelerate Performance*. New York: Free Press.

Flade, P., Asplund, J., & Elliot, G. (2015). Employees Who Use Their Strengths Outperform Those Who Don't. *Gallup News*. Retrieved from https://news.gallup.com/businessjournal/186044/employees-strengths-outperform-don.aspx

Frase, Larry E. (1992). *Maximizing People Power in Schools: Motivating and Managing Teachers and Staff*. Newbury Park, CA: Corwin Press, Inc.

Gable, S. (2007). People with Cheerleader-Partners Report High Relationship Satisfaction. *APA Brief* Vol. 38, No. 1.

Gallo, Carmino (2016). The 5 Storytellers you will meet in Business. *Forbes*. Retrieved from www.forbes.com/sites/carminegallo/2016/03/18/the-5-storytellers-youll-meet-in-business/#728e10a670cc

Glatthorn, Allen A., & Linda E. Fox (1996). *Quality Teaching Through Professional Development*. Thousand Oaks, CA: Corwin Press, Inc.

Gokce, Fuat (2010). Assessment of Teacher Motivation. *School Leadership & Management*, Vol. 30, No. 5, pp. 487–499.

Green-Reese, S., Johnson, D. J., & Campbell, W. A. (1991). Teacher Job Satisfaction and Teacher Job Stress: School Size, Age and Teaching Experience. *Education* Vol. 112, No. 2, pp. 247–252.

Hargreaves, A. (1998). The Emotional Practice of Teaching. *Teaching and Teacher Education* Vol. 14, pp. 835–854. doi:10.1016/s0742-051x(98)00025–0

Harris, B. (2017). More Teachers Are Taking Second Jobs to Make Ends Meet. *US News*. Retrieved from www.usnews.com/news/best-states/mississippi/articles/2017-12-16/more-teachers-are-taking-second-jobs-to-make-ends-meet

Heathfield, S. (2016). The 5 Teams that Every Organization Needs Your Organization's Needs for Teams Will Vary but These Will Get You Started. Retrieved from www.thebalancecareers.com/the-5-teams-that-every-organization-needs-1918507

Hodges, Diane (2004). *Looking Forward to Monday Morning: Ideas for Recognition and Appreciation Activities and Fun Things to Do at Work for Educators*. New York: Corwin Press, Inc.

Hodges, Diane (2013). Teacher Appreciation: Nine Recognition Tips and Ideas. *Communicator*. Retrieved from https://www.naesp.org/communicator-may-2013/teacher-appreciation-nine-recognition-tips-and-ideas

Hoerr, Thomas R. (2008). What Is Instructional Leadership? *Educational Leadership* Vol. 65, No. 4, pp. 84–85.

Ingersoll, R. (2001). The Status of Teaching as a Profession. Retrieved from https://repository.upenn.edu/cgi/viewcontent.cgi?referer=&httpsredir=1&article=1226&context=gse_pubs

Jacob, Brian, & Lefgren, Lars (2007). What Do Parents Value in Education? An Empirical Investigation of Parents' Revealed Preferences for Teachers. *The Quarterly Journal of Economics, MIT Press* Vol. 122, No. 4, pp. 1603–1637, November.

Johnson, Brad, & Jones, Melody (2017). *Learning on Your Feet: Incorporating Physical Activity into the K-8 Classroom*. New York: Routledge.

Johnson, Brad, & McElroy, Tammy (2010). *The Edutainer: Connecting the Art and Science of Teaching*. Lanham, MD: Rowman & Littlefield.

Johnson, Brad, & Sessions, Julie (2016). *From School Administrator to School Leader: 15 keys to Maximizing your Leadership Potential*. New York: Routledge.

Johnson, Brad, & Zimmerman, Marty (2018). *Call for Leadership: Effective Practices of Leaders in Search for New Wisdom*. New York: Rowman & Littlefield.

Johnson, Sarah (1986). Incentives for Teachers: What Motivates, What Matters. *Educational Administration Quarterly* Vol. 22, No. 3(Summer), pp. 54–79.

Kubicek, J. (2015). *5 Gears: How to Be Present and Productive When There Is Never Enough Time*. New York: Wiley.

Lencioni, P. (2002). *The Five Dysfunctions of a Team: A Leadership Fable*. San Francisco, CA: Jossey-Bass.

Lipkin, Nicole (2017). Interview with School Leaders Now. Retrieved from https://schoolleadersnow.weareteachers.com/little-ways-boost-teacher-morale/

Little, J. W. (1982). Norms of Collegiality and Experimentation: Workplace Conditions of School Success. *American Educational Research Journal* Vol. 19, No. 3, p. 333.

Long, Cindy (2012). Bullying of Teachers Pervasive in Many Schools. *NEA Today*. Retrieved from http://neatoday.org/2012/05/16/bullying-of-teachers-pervasive-in-many-schools-2/

Metlife Survey of the American Teacher (2012). Retrieved from www.metlife.com/content/dam/microsites/about/corporate-profile/MetLife-Teacher-Survey-2012.pdf

Minarik, M. M., Thornton, B., & Perreault, G. (2003). Systems Thinking can Improve Teacher Retention. *Clearing House* Vol. 76, No. 5, pp. 230–234.

Nayer, V. (2010). *Employees First, Customers Second*. Boston, MA: Harvard Business Review Press.

O'Neil, F. H., & Drillings, M. (1995). *Motivation: Theory and Research*. Hillsdale, NJ: Lawrence Erlbaum Ass.

Peterson, Kenneth D. (1995). *Teacher Evaluation: A Comprehensive Guide to New Directions and Practices*. Thousand Oaks, CA: Corwin Press, Inc.

Pink, D. (2011). *Drive: The Surprising Truth About What Motivates*. New York: Riverhead Books.

Rath, T., & Clifton, D. O. (2004). *How Full Is Your Bucket? Positive Strategies for Work and Life*. New York: Gallup Press.

Roak, Theresa (2017, October 29). Personal/Email Interview.

Robertson, R. (2017, November 20). Personal/Email Interview.

Rosenthal, Lauren (2017). 5 Little Ways to Boost Teacher Morale and Get Big Results School *Leaders Now*. Retrieved from https://

schoolleadersnow.weareteachers.com/little-ways-boost-teacher-morale/

Rosenthal, N. (2012). 10 Ways to Enhance Your Emotional Intelligence. *Psychology Today*. Retrieved from www.psychologytoday.com/us/blog/your-mind-your-body/201201/10-ways-enhance-your-emotional-intelligence

Rubin, R. (2002). Will the Real SMART Goals Please Stand Up? *Science for a Smarter Workplace*. Retrieved from www.siop.org/tip/backissues/tipapr02/03rubin.aspx

Ruth, Babe quote (2016). Retrieved from www.inc.com/gordon-tredgold/50-quotes-on-the-importance-and-benefits-of-teamwork.html

Sahlberg, P. (2011). *Finnish Lessons: What Can the World Learn from Educational Change in Finland?* New York: Teachers College Press.

School Leaders Network (2014). Churn: The High Cost of Principal Turnover. Retrieved from https://connectleadsucceed.org/sites/default/files/principal_turnover_cost.pdf

Seashore Louis, K., Leithwood, K., & Anderson, S. (2010). *Learning from Leadership Project: Investigating the Links to Improved Student Learning*. Minneapolis: Center for Applied Research and Educational Improvement, University of Minnesota.

Sebring, P. B., & Bryk, A. S. (2000). School Leadership and the Bottom Line in Chicago. *Phi Delta Kappan* Vol. 81, No. 6, pp. 440–443.

Smith, J. (2013). 10 Reasons Why Humor Is a Key to Success at Work. *Forbes*. Retrieved from www.forbes.com/sites/jacquelynsmith/2013/05/03/10-reasons-why-humor-is-a-key-to-success-at-work/#61d3f1bf5c90

Stone, Howard, Parker, James D. A., & Wood, Laura M. (2005). Report on the Ontario Principals' Council Leadership Study. Retrieved from www.eiconsortium.org/pdf/opc_leadership_study_final_report.pdf

Strauss, V. (2013). What if Finland's great teachers taught in U.S. schools? *Washington Post*. Retrieved from www.washingtonpost.com/news/answer-sheet/wp/2013/05/15/what-if-finlands-great-teachers-taught-in-u-s-schools-not-what-you-think/?utm_term=.a443495a854d

Swartz, K. (2014). What Motivates Teachers? *MindShift*. Retrieved from www.kqed.org/mindshift/36924/what-motivates-teachers).

TALIS (2013). The OECD Teaching and Learning International Survey. Retrieved from www.oecd.org/finland/TALIS-2013-country-note-Finland.pdf

Trampe, D., Quoidbach J., & Taquet, M. (2015). Emotions in Everyday Life. *PloS One* Vol. 10, No. 12, p. e0145450.

Tredgold, Gordon (2016). 50 Quotes on the Importance of Collaboration and Cooperation in Teamwork. *INC.* Retrieved from https://www.inc.com/gordon-tredgold/50-quotes-on-the-importance-and-benefits-of-teamwork.html

Verdugo, R., & Schneider, J. (1999). Quality Schools, Safe Schools: A Theoretical and Empirical Discussion. *Education and Urban Society* Vol. 31, No. 3, pp. 286–307.

Wood, Alex, et al. (2009). Gratitude and well-Being: A Review and Theoretical Integration. *Clinical Psychology Review* pp. 16, December.

Young, Mitch (2017, December 6). Personal Interview.

Zenger, J., & Folkman, J. et al. (2012). *How to Be Exceptional: Drive Leadership Success by Magnifying Your Strengths.* New York: McGraw-Hill.

Online Sources

www.americanprogress.org/issues/education-k-12/reports/2014/07/09/93104/return-on-educational-investment-2/

www.ascd.org/publications/educational-leadership/apr15/vol72/num07/Good-Ways-to-Communicate-with-Teachers.aspx

www.ascd.org/publications/educational-leadership/feb14/vol71/num05/An-Open-Letter-on-Teacher-Morale.aspx

https://blog.cetrain.isu.edu/blog/5-leadership-qualities-we-learned-from-walt-disney

https://blog.schoolrunner.org/communication-between-school-leaders-and-teachers/

www.businessnewsdaily.com/3699-healthy-eating-worker-productivity.html

www.cashort.com/blog/5-tips-to-create-a-culture-of-appreciation-in-the-workplace

www.chalkbeat.org/posts/co/2017/01/20/teacher-by-day-waitress-by-night-colorado-teachers-work-second-jobs-to-make-ends-meet/

www.curriculumcrafter.com/2016/05/10/10-reasons-teachers-deserve-celebrated/

www.davidgeurin.com/2016/01/7-trust-building-behaviors-teachers.html

www.educationworld.com/a_admin/admin/admin538.shtml

http://edge.ascd.org/blogpost/10-simple-ways-for-principals-to-show-teachers-appreciation

www.edsurge.com/news/2016-06-28-5-things-teachers-want-from-pd-and-how-coaching-and-collaboration-can-deliver-them-if-implementation-improves

www.eiconsortium.org/pdf/opc_leadership_study_final_report.pdf

www.employeeconnect.com/blog/12-powerful-tips-build-employee-recognition-culture/

www.edutopia.org/blog/proposals-for-improving-teacher-morale-terry-heick

www.fearlessmotivation.com/2016/05/30/11-inspiring-walt-disney-quotes-ignite-imagination/

https://fillingmymap.com/2015/04/15/11-ways-finlands-education-system-shows-us-that-less-is-more/

www.forbes.com/forbes/2006/1225/033.html#2082491c4b15

www.forbes.com/sites/carminegallo/2016/03/18/the-5-storytellers-youll-meet-in-business/#728e10a670cc (Branson)

http://news.gallup.com/poll/161516/teachers-love-lives-struggle-workplace.aspx

http://news.gallup.com/opinion/gallup/183398/don-wait-until-school-year-end-recognize-teachers.aspx

www.gallup.com/services/176741/principal-talent-seen-teachers-eyes.aspx

http://go.globoforce.com/rs/862-JIQ-698/images/ROIofRecognition.pdf

www.goldmansachs.com/our-thinking/talks-at-gs/dan-schulman.html

https://greatergood.berkeley.edu/pdfs/GratitudePDFs/2Wood-GratitudeWell-BeingReview.pdf

http://hechingerreport.org/why-do-more-than-half-of-principals-quit-after-five-years/

www.inc.com/sujan-patel/20-creative-ways-to-boost-employee-morale.html

https://institutesuccess.com/library/communication-the-human-connection-is-the-key-to-personal-and-career-success-paul-j-meyer/

www.kqed.org/mindshift/36924/what-motivates-teachers

http://leadingwithintent.com/.

www.mouseplanet.com/8210/Walts_Favorite_Teacher_Daisy_Beck

www.naesp.org/sites/default/files/resources/2/Principal/2007/J-Fp48.pdf

www.naesp.org/sites/default/files/resources/2/Principal/2007/S-Op16.pdf

www.nde-ed.org/TeachingResources/ClassroomTips/Teamwork.htm (NDT Resource)

www.nycleadershipacademy.org/news-and-resources/tools-and-publications/pdfs/teaming-white-paper

www.raiseyourhandtexas.org/stories/smith-elementary/?utm

www.researchgate.net/publication/237469096_The_Beliefs_Practices_and_Computer_Use_of_Teacher_Leaders1

www.sargentshriver.org/speech-article/the-hardest-job-in-america

https://schoolleadersnow.weareteachers.com/little-ways-boost-teacher-morale/

www.theatlantic.com/education/archive/2014/07/why-poor-schools-cant-win-at-standardized-testing/374287/

www.theguardian.com/education/2015/jun/17/highly-trained-respected-and-free-why-finlands-teachers-are-different

www.weareteachers.com/teach-to-your-strengths/